EXPOSED AND EMPOWERED

WHEN GOD LOWER THE HEDGE

MICHELLE BARKER

CONTENTS

Description

"Exposed and Empowered: When God Lowers the Hedge"

What if the trials you're facing are not the end, but a new beginning?

Have you ever felt God's protection so strongly, only to wake up one day and feel completely exposed? In this book *"Exposed and Empowered: When God Lowers the Hedge,"* discover the untold truth behind those moments when God's divine barrier seems to vanish, and life's storms hit hard.

This isn't just another book about faith; it's an invitation to understand God's deeper work in your life. Through powerful biblical insights, raw stories, and real-life applications, this book unpacks why God allows His hedge of protection to be lowered and how these seasons of challenge are actually refining moments, designed to strengthen your faith and draw you closer to Him.

Allow these heart-stirring words to guide you through the valleys of uncertainty, showing you how to stand firm on God's Word, recognize His hand at work even in the struggle, and find the courage to keep moving forward. This book isn't just about surviving your trials; it's about thriving through them and discovering a deeper relationship with God than you ever thought possible.

When God Lowers the Hedge is not just a message; it's a lifeline of hope. Dive in, and find out why the moments when God seems silent are often the very moments He's setting you up for your greatest breakthrough. Are you ready to see the beauty behind the battle? Your journey to spiritual growth and unshakeable faith starts here.

Introduction

"Exposed and Empowered: When God Lowers the Hedge"

Imagine for a second that your life is like a garden; full of promise, beauty, and loaded with potential. Like any garden, it needs protection from all kinds of things; the harsh weather, pests, or anything that might mess up its growth. Now, picture God putting a hedge around this garden; a divine fence that keeps out anything that could harm you, letting you grow and thrive in peace. But what happens when that hedge gets lowered? Suddenly, your garden is exposed to storms, wild animals, and all the unpredictable elements life can throw at you.

That's exactly what this book, **"Exposed and Empowered: When God Lowers the Hedge,"** is all about. It's a question we've all asked at one point, especially in those tough times: Why, after feeling God's favor and protection for so long, does it suddenly feel like everything's going wrong? Why does God let us go through pain, struggles, and challenges when He's been keeping us safe all this time?

The idea of a "hedge" of protection goes way back. In ancient times, people would put thick, thorny hedges around their vineyards and crops to keep out wild animals and thieves. Spiritually speaking, this hedge is like God's personal security system over your life; keeping you safe from dangers you can see and those you can't. It's not just about protecting you physically; it's about guarding your heart, mind, and spirit, too.

But here's the thing; sometimes, God allows that hedge to come down. Now, this isn't God being cruel or careless. It's part of His bigger plan; a plan that often includes refining us, testing our faith, and ultimately making us stronger. The Bible is packed with stories of people who had their hedge lowered; Job, Joseph, David, and so many others; yet they came out the other side with a deeper faith, a stronger understanding of God's love, and a clearer sense of His purpose.

"Exposed and Empowered: When God Lowers the Hedge" will take you through the what, when, how, and who of God's hedge of protection. We'll dig into what this divine barrier really means, how it operates, and why sometimes it feels like it's gone. We'll look at the conditions that keep the hedge up and the reasons why God might choose to lower it, showing us that it's all part of His grand design for our lives.

This book isn't just about diving deep into theology; it's a practical guide, meant to make you think, challenge what you know, and push you closer to God. Whether you're in the middle of a storm right now or just curious about how God's protection works, this book will give you the tools and insights you need to navigate your faith journey.

You'll come to see that when the hedge is lowered, it's not something to be scared of. It's an opportunity; an open door to grow, to trust God in new ways, and to see His hand at work in ways you never dreamed of. Through these pages, you'll learn what to do—and what not to do—when you find yourself exposed. You'll discover how to walk through those times and come out stronger, wiser, and more grounded in your faith.

As we take this journey together, I'm inviting you to open your heart and your mind to the idea that God's protection isn't just about shielding you from trouble. It's about getting you ready for something greater. When God lowers the hedge, it's not the end of His protection; it's the start of a brand-new chapter in your spiritual walk. A chapter full of growth, purpose, and the unshakeable assurance that His love is with you, no matter what.

Welcome to **"Exposed and Empowered: When God Lowers the Hedge."** Let's take this journey together and see where God leads us.

Dedication

To those who have walked through the storms of life,
and found God's protection in the midst of the trial.
This book is dedicated to you.
May you always find your refuge in Him.

"The name of the Lord is a strong tower;
The righteous run to it and are safe."
— Proverbs 18:10 (NKJV)

"The Lord is my rock and my fortress and my deliverer;
My God, my strength, in whom I will trust;
My shield and the horn of my salvation, my stronghold."
— Psalm 18:2 (NKJV)

PREFACE

HEDGE DEFINITION

The Hebrew word commonly translated as *"hedge"* in the Bible is **(suk or sukh)**, which primarily means to fence, enclose, cover, or protect. This word conveys the idea of setting up a protective barrier, something that surrounds and keeps safe.

Key Hebrew Definitions of "Hedge" (suk):

1. **To Fence In or Enclose:** The word suggests putting up a protective wall or barrier that separates and secures what is inside from external threats. It's like setting up a stronghold or defense around something valuable.

2. **To Protect or Guard:** It reflects the action of guarding something precious, ensuring its safety from harm, whether that harm is physical, spiritual, or emotional.

3. **To Block or Restrain:** It also carries the connotation of preventing access or keeping things out, such as dangers, enemies,

or unwanted influences. This can be seen as both a protective measure and a means of maintaining boundaries.

Biblical Context:

- **Job 1:10** is one of the best examples where this concept is used: *"Have You not made a **hedge** around him, around his household, and around all that he has on every side?"* This illustrates God's divine protection and favor over Job, encompassing his entire life.

- The "hedge" is more than a physical boundary; it's symbolic of God's encompassing care, protection, and divine favor. It implies that God Himself acts as a shield around His people, blocking out harm and preserving them.

The word "suk" encapsulates the idea of God's protective covering, emphasizing His active role in guarding and preserving those who trust in Him.

CHAPTER ONE

GOD'S HEDGE OF PROTECTION

UNDERSTANDING THE HEDGE

Ever wonder what it really means when we talk about God putting a "hedge" around us? In the Bible, a hedge wasn't just some cute little garden fence. It was serious business, a thick, thorny barrier that kept the bad stuff out. Think of it like a natural wall made of brambles, keeping the wolves away from your sheep and the thieves out of your vineyard. Back in the day, these hedges protected crops, livestock, and people's livelihoods from anything that meant harm.

Now, spiritually speaking, the Bible takes this idea and flips it into something way deeper: God's hedge is like that invisible shield He puts around us to keep us safe from all kinds of mess. But what does that look like in real life? And why do we need it so much?

The Biblical Foundation

If you've ever heard of Job, you know his story is all about God's protection and what happens when that protection gets lowered. In Job 1:10 (NKJV), the devil himself tells God:

"Have You not made a hedge around him, around his household, and around all that he has on every side? You have blessed the work of his hands, and his possessions have increased in the land."

That hedge around Job was like God saying, "Nah, you can't touch him." Job's life was blessed; his family was straight, his money was good, and his health was on point. But then, God allowed that hedge to come down for a moment, and all hell broke loose. Job's story shows us that this divine protection isn't a promise that bad things won't ever happen; it's a reminder that God has His hand on us, and nothing can touch us without His say-so.

Protection in Various Forms

God's hedge isn't always about keeping us safe from physical harm. It's not just about protecting your body; it's about protecting your mind, your heart, and your soul too. Sometimes it looks like that job opportunity you got that you weren't even qualified for, or that close call you had when you almost got into a car accident but somehow didn't. Other times, it's God keeping you from making that call you'd regret or protecting your spirit from falling into depression or temptation.

Psalm 91:1-4 (NKJV) breaks it down like this:

"He who dwells in the secret place of the Most High shall abide under the shadow of the Almighty. I will say of the Lord, 'He is my refuge and my fortress; My God, in Him I will trust.' Surely He shall deliver you from the snare of the fowler and from the perilous pestilence. He shall cover you with His feathers, and under His wings you shall take refuge; His truth shall be your shield and buckler."

It's God saying, "I got you." No matter what the world throws at you, there's safety, peace, and covering under His wings. It's like having a spiritual force field around you that shields you from what you can see and even what you can't.

Why We Need the Hedge

Let's be real, life's tough out here. There's danger, there's drama, and let's not even get started on the spiritual battles we face every day. 1 Peter 5:8 (NKJV) keeps it straight with us:

"Be sober, be vigilant; because your adversary the devil walks about like a roaring lion, seeking whom he may devour."

That's why God's hedge is so crucial. Without it, we're sitting ducks for all kinds of attacks. The hedge doesn't mean you won't go through things, but it means that whatever comes your way has already been filtered through God's hands. And if He's allowing it, you best believe there's a purpose behind it.

But let's not get it twisted, the hedge isn't just this magic wall that stays up no matter what. It's dynamic. It can be strong or weak, depending on how close we are to God, how obedient we are, and how often we're leaning on Him. Throughout the Bible, you see times when God protects His people fiercely. But when they stray, turn their backs, and do their own thing, sometimes that hedge gets lowered. In Isaiah 5:5 (NKJV), God says:

"And now, please let Me tell you what I will do to My vineyard: I will take away its hedge, and it shall be burned; and break down its wall, and it shall be trampled down."

God's protection isn't conditional on His love; it's always there. But the fullness of His protection? That can depend on whether we're living inside His will or doing our own thing. It's like having an umbrella; it doesn't do you any good if you step outside it when it's pouring rain.

A Call to Reflection

So, as you think about this hedge of protection, it's worth asking yourself: Where am I standing? Am I under God's protection, or am I flirting with danger by stepping outside His boundaries? Are you living in a way that says, "God, I trust you," or are you testing His limits?

In the next chapters, we're going to dig even deeper into this concept; looking at when the hedge is present, how it operates, and what happens when it's lowered. But for now, take a second to think about how God's been hedging you in ways you might not have even noticed.

Maybe you've been protected from a relationship that would've broken you, or perhaps God kept you from taking that job that seemed perfect but would've led you away from Him. The hedge is about more than just safety; it's about God's plan, His timing, and His way of working all things together for your good, even when you can't see it.

And if you're wondering, "What if God lowers the hedge in my life?" Just remember this: Even when the hedge is down, God is still up to something. He's not abandoning you; He's shaping you, guiding you, and leading you into something greater. So, trust the process and keep your faith strong, because God's got you covered, hedge or no hedge.

CHAPTER TWO

THE PURPOSE OF THE HEDGE

WHY GOD PLACES THE HEDGE

God's hedge of protection is one of the most loving and powerful things He does for us. This hedge shows us who God is; His love, His grace, and His deep desire to guide us along the right path. So, why does God put this hedge around us? What's the real purpose behind it, and what does it say about who He is?

This chapter dives into why God's hedge is so important in our lives. It's not just a wall of protection; it's a sign of His care, His guidance, and His desire to keep us on track with the plans He has for us. Let's explore why this hedge is so critical to our spiritual walk and what it reveals about God's bigger picture.

Protection as an Expression of Love

God's hedge is His way of saying, "I love you." Just like parents keep their kids safe from harm, God uses this hedge to shield us from all kinds of trouble. It's not just about keeping our bodies safe but also our hearts, minds, and souls.

In Psalm 91:14-16 (NKJV), God promises:

"Because he has set his love upon Me, therefore I will deliver him; I will set him on high, because he has known My name. He shall call upon Me, and I will answer him; I will be with him in trouble; I will deliver him and honor him. With long life I will satisfy him, and show him My salvation."

This passage is God saying, "I've got you." The hedge is more than just a barrier; it's a sign of His love and commitment to those who trust in Him. It's like a parent keeping a watchful eye on their child, ready to step in and protect them at any moment.

Guidance and Discipline

Sometimes God's hedge isn't just about protection; it's also about direction. It's like God's way of nudging us back on track when we start wandering off. Think of it like bumpers in a bowling alley; they're there to keep the ball (that's us) from going into the gutter. When we're off course, God uses His hedge to guide us back to His will.

Proverbs 3:11-12 (NKJV) tells us:

"My son, do not despise the chastening of the Lord, nor detest His correction; for whom the Lord loves He corrects, just as a father the son in whom he delights."

God's hedge can be a form of discipline, not just from outside threats but also from ourselves. It's like when you're about to make a decision that would mess everything up, and suddenly something stops you. That's God keeping you from self-sabotage. He's looking out for us, even when we don't realize we need it.

You might ask, "Why would God let His hedge down when we mess up?" It's not about punishment; it's about correction. God wants us to get back on track, just like He did with Israel. When they followed Him, He blessed them and kept them safe. But when they turned their backs on Him, He let them feel the weight of their choices, hoping they'd turn back to Him.

Nurturing Faith and Dependence

One of the biggest reasons for God's hedge is to grow our faith and dependence on Him. When we see that our protection comes from God and not ourselves, it builds our trust in Him. It's like realizing you don't have to have all the answers because God's got it covered.

Jesus puts it plainly in John 15:5 (NKJV):

"I am the vine, you are the branches. He who abides in Me, and I in him, bears much fruit; for without Me you can do nothing."

This verse hits home because it's a reminder that without God, we're powerless. The hedge keeps us close to Him, connected like branches to a vine. It's His way of saying, "Stay close, and you'll be okay." It's not just about avoiding harm; it's about building a deep, real relationship with God, one that keeps us grounded and strong.

Preservation of Purpose

God didn't just put us here to take up space; each of us has a unique purpose, a calling that only we can fulfill. His hedge helps us stay on the path that leads to that purpose. It's like a GPS that reroutes us when we take the wrong turn, making sure we still get to where we need to be.

Jeremiah 29:11 (NKJV) is a verse that speaks to this:

"For I know the thoughts that I think toward you, says the Lord, thoughts of peace and not of evil, to give you a future and a hope."

God's hedge is all about preserving that hope and future **He has planned for you**. It's there to protect your dreams, your mission, and the work **He's called you to do**. The hedge isn't just about keeping things out; it's also about keeping you on track, making sure nothing messes with your God-given destiny.

A Testament to God's Sovereignty

Finally, the hedge is a straight-up reminder that God is in control. He's not just watching from the sidelines; He's actively involved, making sure nothing happens outside of His will. When God puts a hedge around us, He's declaring that He's the boss; He's got the final say over our lives.

Psalm 121:7-8 (NKJV) beautifully sums this up:

"The Lord shall preserve you from all evil; He shall preserve your soul. The Lord shall preserve your going out and your coming in from this time forth, and even forevermore."

These words remind us that God's protection is ongoing, not just a one-time deal. It's a constant, faithful assurance that He's got our backs from the moment we wake up to the time we lay down. The hedge is a powerful symbol of God's sovereignty and His loving control over our lives.

Reflecting on the Purpose

As you wrap up this chapter, take a moment to think about how God's hedge has been active in your life:

- How has He protected you when you didn't even know you needed it?

- In what ways has He guided you, kept you on track, and nurtured your faith?

- Have you seen His hedge preserving your purpose and keeping you focused on what He's called you to do?

Understanding the purpose of the hedge is key to appreciating how God works in our lives. It's more than just a spiritual shield; it's God's way of drawing us closer, keeping us aligned with His will, and ensuring that we fulfill the incredible plans He has for us. As we continue this journey, we'll dig deeper into what happens when the hedge is lifted and how we can respond in faith and trust. But for now, let's hold onto the truth that God's hedge is not just a barrier; it's a sign of His deep love, guidance, and purpose, calling us to trust Him more each day.

CHAPTER THREE

THE CONDITIONS OF THE HEDGE

THE DEEP CONNECTION BETWEEN OBEDIENCE AND GOD'S PROTECTION

Let's get one thing straight: God's hedge of protection isn't just some random thing He throws out there whenever He feels like it. It's deeply connected to our relationship with Him, especially our obedience. You see, throughout the Bible, God's protection is always wrapped up in a relationship, one where we're walking closely with Him, listening to His voice, and following His ways. When we stick with God, His hedge is strong, covering us from all sides. But when we start doing our own thing, stepping outside of His commands, that hedge can start to weaken, leaving us wide open to all kinds of mess we were never meant to deal with.

This chapter dives deep into what keeps that hedge tight around us and what can cause it to start falling apart. Because once you understand the conditions of God's protection, you can learn to live safely in His care, avoiding the pitfalls that can leave you exposed.

Covenant Relationship: The Foundation of God's Protection

It all starts with covenant; God's promise to protect, bless, and keep us when we stay in right relationship with Him. A covenant isn't just some casual agreement; it's a divine contract, an unbreakable bond where God says, "I've got you, but you've got to stay true to Me." From the Old Testament to the New, God made it clear that His protection is reserved for those who are committed to Him, those who are willing to walk in His ways.

Look at what God told Israel in Deuteronomy 28:1-2 (NKJV):

"Now it shall come to pass, if you diligently obey the voice of the Lord your God, to observe carefully all His commandments which I command you today, that the Lord your God will set you high above all nations of the earth. And all these blessings shall come upon you and overtake you, because you obey the voice of the Lord your God."

This isn't a vague promise; it's specific. God is saying, "If you obey Me, I'll bless you beyond measure. My protection will be all over you." Obedience is like the glue that keeps God's hedge in place. When we follow His commands, we're not just doing what's right; we're securing His protection over every part of our lives. It's a divine exchange: stay faithful to God, and He'll keep you covered.

Faithfulness and Devotion: God Wants Your Heart

But God isn't just looking for obedience on the outside; He wants our heart. He's looking for folks who are truly devoted to Him, not just ticking off boxes on a religious checklist. Faithfulness is about more than doing the right things; it's about loving God with everything you've got; seeking Him first, putting Him above everything else, and living in a way that reflects His character to the world.

2 Chronicles 16:9 (NKJV) breaks it down:

"For the eyes of the Lord run to and fro throughout the whole earth, to show Himself strong on behalf of those whose heart is loyal to Him."

Again, God is searching; always looking for hearts that are fully committed to Him. And when He finds someone who's loyal, someone who doesn't back down when things get hard, He shows up in a big way. That loyalty is like a fortress around you, keeping the hedge strong even when life tries to break you down. A devoted heart doesn't waver when the storm hits; it digs in deeper, knowing that God is right there in the midst of it all.

Living Under the Hedge: More Than Just Rules

Obedience and faithfulness aren't about living under a set of strict rules just to keep God happy. It's about aligning yourself with His best for your life. God's commands aren't random; they're designed to keep you safe, to bless you, and to guide you through whatever comes your way. When you live in obedience, you're not just following orders; you're positioning yourself to experience God's protection in full effect. And when your heart is faithful, God's favor surrounds you like a shield, keeping you covered even when the enemy tries to come for you.

So, don't just follow God halfway. Don't live with one foot inside the hedge and the other out in the world. We call that straddling the fence. Step fully into God's promises by living a life of obedience and devotion. Because when you do, you're not just staying safe; you're living in the fullness of everything God has for you. You're living protected, blessed, and firmly under the watchful eye of the One who loves you more than you could ever imagine.

The Power of Prayer: Your Lifeline to God's Protection

Prayer is more than just a routine or a quick check-in with God when things are rough; it's your hotline straight to heaven, a life-line that keeps you anchored when life feels like it's spinning out of control. It's like having God on speed dial, ready to step into your situation at a moment's notice. But let's get one thing clear: prayer isn't just about asking God for stuff; it's about connection, dependence, and inviting Him into every corner of your life. It's that moment when you stop everything else and just say, "God, I need You right here, right now."

Philippians 4:6-7 (NKJV) breaks it down perfectly:

"Be anxious for nothing, but in everything by prayer and supplication, with thanksgiving, let your requests be made known to God; and the peace

of God, which surpasses all understanding, will guard your hearts and minds through Christ Jesus."

You see, prayer isn't just about moving God's hand; it's about moving our hearts closer to His. It's that divine exchange where you pour out your worries, your fears, and your needs, and God responds with peace that doesn't even make sense to the world. That's what's so powerful; it's peace that stands guard like a soldier at your heart's door, refusing to let anxiety, fear, or doubt take over. That peace is what keeps the hedge strong even when life is throwing punches. It's like God saying, "I got this. Just keep talking to Me. Keep that line open, and watch what I'll do."

Righteous Living: Aligning with God's Shield

Now, prayer might be your lifeline, but righteous living is like the reinforcement that keeps that hedge fortified. Living righteously means living right; honoring God in what you do, say, and even think. It's about showing up every day, doing your best to reflect God's heart, and treating people with the same grace God shows you. Righteous living isn't about being perfect; it's about striving to do what's right and repenting when you fall short.

Psalm 5:12 (NKJV) lays it out:

"For You, O Lord, will bless the righteous; with favor You will surround him as with a shield."

Let that sink in. God's favor surrounds the righteous like a shield. That's another picture of the hedge; God's protective favor encircling you, keeping you safe, and showing up in ways that don't even make sense sometimes. And don't get it twisted; God's not asking you to have it all together. It's not about perfection, it's about direction. It's about making a genuine effort to live right, to treat people right, and to walk in a way that honors God. When you do that, God's favor isn't just something you hope for; it's something you walk in daily.

Prayer and Righteous Living: A Dynamic Duo

Prayer and righteous living go hand in hand. One without the other is like having a car with no fuel or a house with no roof. You can pray all day, but if you're living wild and reckless, those prayers are like seeds thrown on rocky ground. And you can live upright, but if you're not praying, you're missing that direct line to God's heart and help. When you combine the two, though? That's when the hedge is at its strongest. That's when you're not just surviving; you're thriving, living under the shield of God's protection with peace that's unshakable. So, keep that prayer line open. Keep living in a way that honors God. Because when you do, you're not just protecting yourself; you're positioning yourself to receive all that God has for you; His peace, His protection, His favor, and His guidance. And that, my friend, is the kind of life that stands firm, no matter what comes your way.

Repentance and Restoration

Let's be real; we all fall short. But the good news is, when we mess up, God doesn't just leave us hanging. Repentance is like hitting the reset button; it's our way of saying, "God, I'm sorry. Help me get back on track." Repentance restores that broken connection and brings the hedge back in place.

1 John 1:9 (NKJV) assures us:

"If we confess our sins, He is faithful and just to forgive us our sins and to cleanse us from all unrighteousness."

When we repent, God not only forgives us, but He also rebuilds the hedge that our sins may have weakened. It's like inviting His protection back into our lives. So, no matter how far we stray, God's always ready to welcome us back and renew His protective care.

The Real Cost of Ignoring God's Conditions

Let's be real; there are consequences when we start living life on our own terms, ignoring God's conditions, and thinking we can handle things our way. Skipping out on prayer, turning our back on righteousness, and refusing to repent are not just small missteps; they're choices that come with a cost. And that cost is often paid with our peace, our protection, and our spiritual strength. When we start doing things outside of God's design, the hedge that's supposed to guard us begins to weaken. That protective barrier that once shielded us from attacks? It's no longer as strong as it used to be, and we find ourselves exposed, vulnerable, and dealing with hardships that God never intended for us.

The Bible doesn't shy away from this truth. Isaiah 59:1-2 (NKJV) lays it out plain:

"Behold, the Lord's hand is not shortened, that it cannot save; nor His ear heavy, that it cannot hear. But your iniquities have separated you from your God; and your sins have hidden His face from you, so that He will not hear."

You feel that? That's the weight of God's Word hitting home. It's not that God's arm isn't strong enough to reach us, and it's not that His ears are clogged up. No, it's our own iniquities—our sins, our stubbornness, our refusal to live right; that build a wall between us and the God who loves us. And let's get one thing straight: God doesn't want to see us struggle. He doesn't delight in watching His children fumble through life without His protection. But when we choose to step outside of His ways, we essentially step outside of His covering.

Choices Have Consequences

We've got to understand that our choices carry weight. Every decision we make, every time we decide to skip prayer, every time we compromise on what we know is right, we're creating cracks in that hedge. It's like walking away from an umbrella in a storm and then wondering why we're getting drenched. God never intended for us to be out here unprotected, battling struggles that we weren't built to fight alone. But when we ignore His conditions; when we refuse to stay in the secret place, when we let sin creep in without repentance; we're the ones stepping outside that divine umbrella.

Let's break this down: God's protection isn't about Him being absent; it's about us being absent-minded to His presence. We can't live like there's no standard, and then be surprised when the enemy starts to have his way. When you ignore God's call to righteousness, you open the door for spiritual attacks. When you neglect repentance, you allow sin to fester, and sin separates. And sin doesn't just separate us from God; it separates us from the peace, the strength, and the confidence that come with knowing we're covered.

A Wake-Up Call

This is a wake-up call, not to condemn, but to correct. If you've been feeling exposed, vulnerable, or like life's been hitting you harder than ever, it might be time to check the condition of your hedge. Have you been praying like you used to? Have you been living righteously, or have you been cutting corners with your faith? Have you been quick to repent, or are you carrying unconfessed sins, hoping God will just overlook them? God is ready and willing to restore, but He's looking for a heart that's willing to return.

Don't let the enemy deceive you into thinking that God's not there. Don't let shame, guilt, or pride keep you from getting back to where you belong; under the protection of God's hedge. You've got to guard your prayer life, protect your righteousness, and stay quick to repent. Because when you do, you're not just maintaining a hedge; you're fortifying your future, securing your peace, and keeping yourself under the watchful care of the One who loves you most.

It's time to come back to the hedge. It's time to make the choices that keep us covered, connected, and confident in God's unbreakable love.

This isn't just about knowing how the hedge works. It's time to look at our lives and ask:

- Am I faithful in my relationship with God?

- Am I living the way He's called me to live?

- Am I staying connected to Him through prayer?

- Am I quick to repent when I mess up?

As we keep exploring, we'll dig into what happens when the hedge gets lowered. It's not always pretty, but it's also an opportunity for growth, faith, and deeper trust in God. But for now, let's focus on what we can do to stay within the hedge, walking in the peace and security that only God can provide.

CHAPTER FOUR

WHEN THE HEDGE IS LOWERED

THE REALITY OF A LOWERED HEDGE

Picture this: You're walking through life feeling blessed, knowing that God's got you covered on every side. You've seen His protection and felt His peace, but then suddenly, it feels like that shield you've depended on is gone. All of a sudden, you're facing trials and struggles like never before, and it feels like you're out in the open with no cover. That's what happens when God lowers His hedge of protection.

In this chapter, we're going to talk about why God sometimes lets that hedge down. It's not to scare you but to help you understand God's bigger picture. Even when it feels like we're left out in the cold, God's still working. We're going to dig into some biblical examples, look at why God might lower the hedge, and talk about how we can respond when we find ourselves in that place.

Biblical Examples of a Lowered Hedge: When God Steps Back to Bring Us Forward

The Bible doesn't shy away from showing us what happens when God lowers His hedge. It's not random or without purpose; it's intentional. God will sometimes step back, not to leave us hanging, but to test us, correct us, or set the stage for something we can't even see yet. These moments are hard, but they're also opportunities for growth, deeper faith, and a closer walk with God. Let's break down a couple of those moments where God lowered the hedge and why He did it.

Job: A Test of Faith

If you know Job's story, then you know he was living the good life. Job had everything you could think of; wealth, a big family, good health, and most importantly, God's hedge of protection all around him. Even the devil himself recognized that Job was covered. Satan pointed it out to God, saying, "Of course Job loves you, look at how protected he is!" Job 1:10 (NKJV) highlights this when Satan questions God, saying:

"Have You not made a hedge around him, around his household, and around all that he has on every side? You have blessed the work of his hands, and his possessions have increased in the land."

Satan was basically calling Job's faith fake, saying that the only reason Job served God was because of the blessings and protection. So God allowed the hedge to be lowered; not because He wanted to hurt Job, but because He knew Job's faith was deeper than just the blessings. He allowed Satan to test Job but put boundaries in place, saying in Job 1:12 (NKJV):

"And the Lord said to Satan, 'Behold, all that he has is in your power; only do not lay a hand on his person.' So Satan went out from the presence of the Lord."

After this, Job's life got turned upside down. He lost everything: his wealth, his kids, even his health took a nosedive. And through it all, Job never cursed God. He questioned, he wrestled with his pain, but he didn't let go of his faith. The hedge was lowered, but Job's relationship with God held him up. And because of his faithfulness, God restored everything Job had lost; and then some. Job's story isn't just about suffering; it's about a faith that's tested and proven real, showing that God's hedge might be lowered, but His love never is.

Israel: A Lesson in Obedience

Israel's story is another example of how God will lower the hedge as a way to correct and realign His people. Time and again, God protected Israel; fighting their battles, providing for them, guiding them every step of the way. But God's protection wasn't a free pass to live however they wanted. It was tied to their obedience. When they were faithful, they were covered. But when they turned their backs on God, worshipping idols and ignoring His commands, God would step back and let them experience the consequences of their choices.

God speaks on this clearly in Isaiah 5:5 (NKJV):

"And now, please let Me tell you what I will do to My vineyard: I will take away its hedge, and it shall be burned; and break down its wall, and it shall be trampled down."

When God removed His hedge from Israel, it wasn't because He stopped loving them. It was a wake-up call. He allowed them to face the consequences of their actions, hoping they'd realize their need to come back to Him. Every time the hedge came down, it was God's way of saying, "I'm still here, but you need to get back in line with Me." It was tough love, a divine correction to bring them back under His care.

Why God Lowers the Hedge: Finding Purpose in the Pain

Listen, y'all, when God lowers that hedge, it ain't just for kicks. God doesn't just drop His protection to watch us struggle. Every single time God allows the hedge to be lowered, there's a reason behind it, and it's always tied to His love and purpose for us. Let's keep it real: none of us like to feel exposed, vulnerable, or like we're catching every dart the enemy throws. But those seasons when the hedge is lowered? That's where the real growth happens. That's where God shows us who He is and who we really are.

Proving Faith Is Real: The Test of Job

Let's talk about Job. When God lowered the hedge around him, it wasn't some cruel punishment; it was a test. Satan came up in God's face saying, "Job only loves You because of all that protection and blessing. Take that away, and watch him fold." And God said, "Alright, let's see." God wasn't just trying to prove something to Satan; He was showing Job; and all of us; that faith isn't about the stuff we have, but about the God we serve.

When God allowed that hedge to be lowered, Job lost everything: his wealth, his family, his health. But even in his deepest pain, Job held on to his faith. He said, "Though He slay me, yet will I trust in Him" (Job 13:15 NKJV). That's real faith. That's faith that's been tested and proven genuine. And because Job stayed faithful, God restored him double. The lowering of the hedge wasn't about breaking Job; it was about building him up in a way that blessings alone never could. Sometimes, God lowers the hedge to show us and everybody else that our faith is not built on stuff but on the solid rock of who He is.

A Wake-Up Call: Israel's Lesson in Obedience

Then you got Israel, God's chosen people. God blessed them, covered them, fought battles for them, but they got too comfortable. They started doing their own thing, worshipping other gods, ignoring His commands. So, God lowered the hedge. He let them face the consequences of their actions, not to destroy them but to call them back to H im.

Isaiah 5:5 puts it out there plain: *"And now, please let Me tell you what I will do to My vineyard: I will take away its hedge, and it shall be burned; and break down its wall, and it shall be trampled down."* God let them feel the weight of their choices. But even then, His heart was for restoration. He wanted them to see that outside of His protection, life gets real messy, real fast. It was tough love, but it was love all the same. God lowered the hedge to bring His people back to their senses, back to His arms.

God's Goal: Restoration, Not Destruction

The bottom line is this: God's goal in lowering the hedge is always restoration. He's not trying to ruin you; He's trying to refine you. He's not trying to break you down; He's building you up. He's showing you what's in your heart, what's in your life, and where He wants to take you next. When God lowers the hedge, it's an opportunity to draw closer to Him, to deepen your faith, and to come out stronger on the other side.

It's in those moments when the protection seems thin that you see God's faithfulness in ways you never could when everything was going right. You get to see how He sustains, how He keeps, how He brings you through. And sometimes, you have to be a little vulnerable, a little exposed, to truly understand just how mighty your God is.

Holding On When the Hedge Is Down

So, if you're going through it right now, if it feels like God's hedge has been lowered and the hits just keep coming, don't lose heart. Don't let the enemy convince you that God's forgotten about you. Instead, lean in. Ask God, "What are You trying to show me in this? What do You want me to learn?"

God's not silent in your struggle; He's speaking through it. And while it might feel like everything's falling apart, remember that God's still got His hand on you. He's still shaping you, growing you, preparing you for what's next. The hedge might be lowered, but it's not gone. God's still in control. So keep the faith, stay obedient, and know that God's working it all out, even when it doesn't look like it. Trust that the God who set the hedge in the first place knows exactly what He's doing; even when the hedge isn't where it used to be.

Hold on, keep pressing, and watch how God turns this test into a testimony.

Reasons Why the Hedge is Lowered

God doesn't just lower the hedge for no reason. There's always a purpose behind it, and it's often to test us, correct us, or set the stage for something greater. Let's break down why God might let that hedge down.

1. Testing and Strengthening of Faith

God might lower the hedge to test and strengthen your faith. Faith that never gets tested is like a muscle that never gets used. It stays weak.

But when you go through tough times, your faith grows deeper and stronger. It's like refining you, making your faith shine like gold.

1 Peter 1:6-7 (NKJV) puts it like this:

"In this you greatly rejoice, though now for a little while, if need be, you have been grieved by various trials, that the genuineness of your faith, being much more precious than gold that perishes, though it is tested by fire, may be found to praise, honor, and glory at the revelation of Jesus Christ."

These trials make our faith real and powerful, leading us to praise God even more.

2. Discipline and Correction

Sometimes, God lowers the hedge to correct us. When we step out of line, allowing us to face the consequences of our actions is a way to pull us back. It's like a parent disciplining a child; not out of anger, but out of love.

Hebrews 12:6 (NKJV) reminds us:

"For whom the Lord loves He chastens, and scourges every son whom He receives."

God's discipline isn't about punishment; it's about guiding us back to the right path. It's His way of saying, "Come back to Me."

3. Fulfillment of a Greater Purpose

Sometimes God is working on something bigger than what we can see. Remember, His ways are higher than our ways, and sometimes what looks like a setback is actually setting the stage for a comeback.

Think about Joseph in the Bible; his brothers sold him into slavery, and it seemed like his life was falling apart. But God was positioning him to save his family and many others from famine. What looked like a lowered hedge was actually part of God's master plan.

How to Respond When the Hedge is Lowered

When you find yourself in that season where God's hedge seems lower, how you respond matters. It's easy to get discouraged or question God, but here's what you can do to keep your faith strong:

1. Hold Fast to Faith

Like Job, hold on to your faith even when it doesn't make sense. You might not understand why God's letting you go through what you're going through, but you can trust that He's still in control.

James 1:2-4 (NKJV) encourages us:

"My brethren, count it all joy when you fall into various trials, knowing that the testing of your faith produces patience. But let patience have its perfect work, that you may be perfect and complete, lacking nothing."

2. Seek God's Guidance

When the hedge is down, press in closer to God. Get into prayer and His Word because He might be trying to teach you something or redirect your steps.

Psalm 119:105 (NKJV) says:

"Your word is a lamp to my feet and a light to my path."

God's Word will guide you, even in the darkest times.

3. Embrace Repentance and Correction

If the hedge is lowered because of something you've done, don't waste time; repent and turn back to God. He's always ready to forgive and restore.

2 Chronicles 7:14 (NKJV) gives us this promise:

"If My people who are called by My name will humble themselves, and pray and seek My face, and turn from their wicked ways, then I will hear from heaven, and will forgive their sin and heal their land."

4. Trust in God's Sovereignty

Above all, trust that God knows what He's doing. Even when it doesn't make sense, believe that He's working things out for your good.

Romans 8:28 (NKJV) reassures us:

"And we know that all things work together for good to those who love God, to those who are the called according to His purpose."

Conclusion: The Purpose Beyond the Hedge

When God lowers the hedge, it's never just to leave us hanging. Whether it's to test our faith, correct our path, or fulfill something greater, God's always got a purpose. It's a call to trust Him deeper, to lean in closer, and to remember that He's with us even when it feels like we're out there on our own.

In the next chapters, we'll talk more about how God's hedge works and how to stay under His protection. But for now, let's learn the lessons from these tough seasons, knowing that God's still got us, even when the hedge is lowered.

CHAPTER FIVE

HOW THE HEDGE OPERATES

THE MECHANICS OF DIVINE PROTECTION

God's hedge of protection isn't just some invisible wall that sits still and quiet. It's alive, active, and always moving to guard us both in the physical and spiritual realms. It's not just a one-size-fits-all shield; it's dynamic, adjusting to what we need, where we are, and what we're going through. In this chapter, we're going to break down how this hedge operates; how God actively protects His people, how angels get involved, and how our prayers and faith play a role in keeping that protection strong.

When you understand how the hedge works, you start to see just how much God cares about every detail of your life. It'll give you the confidence to walk boldly within His divine protection.

The Role of God's Sovereignty

At the center of it all is God's sovereignty; He's the One in charge. God is not just watching over us; He's actively and carefully orchestrating the hedge around us, deciding when to lift it, when to strengthen it, and when to let it down a bit. Like the perfect gardener He is, it's all according to His perfect wisdom and plan for our lives.

Psalm 91:1-2 (NKJV) captures this perfectly:

"He who dwells in the secret place of the Most High shall abide under the shadow of the Almighty. I will say of the Lord, 'He is my refuge and my fortress; My God, in Him I will trust.'"

When we make our home in God's presence, we put ourselves under His protective shadow. It's like being wrapped up in His arms. God's sovereignty means He's got the final say over our protection. He's constantly adjusting the hedge, keeping it just right for whatever we're facing.

The Activity of Angels: God's First Responders on the Scene

Let's break this down: angels aren't just floating around heaven, playing harps, and looking pretty. Nah, they're God's frontline, His messengers, warriors, and protectors all rolled into one. When we talk about God's hedge of protection, it's not just some invisible force; it's got power, action, and heavenly fire power behind it. And that's where angels come in. They're God's special agents, always on call, ready to guard, guide, and fight for you when the battle gets real
.

Psalm 34:7 sets it straight: *"The angel of the Lord encamps all around those who fear Him, and delivers them."* Think about that. It doesn't just say angels are watching over you from a distance. No, they're setting up camp around you, living right where you live, staying close enough to catch every move the enemy tries to make. Angels are on guard 24/7, patrolling, standing watch, and keeping a lookout so that you don't even see half the mess they're blocking on your behalf.

Picture it: God's got His angels camping around you like an army, tents pitched, swords drawn, eyes wide open. They're not chilling; they're actively engaged, surrounding you with protection and delivering you from danger. And you don't even have to see it to know it's real; God's got His angels out here working overtime to keep you safe, snatching you from harm you didn't even know was coming. When the enemy tries to creep, God's angels are already one step ahead, handling it before it ever reaches you.

Now, let's take it to the New Testament. Hebrews 1:14 tells us straight: *"Are they not all ministering spirits sent forth to minister for those who will inherit salvation?"* Angels are on assignment, specifically dispatched for you, to cover you and make sure you're good. They're not random, aimless beings; they've got orders from the Most High, and those orders are all about keeping you under God's hedge.

Angels minister to us in ways we don't even realize. They show up in moments when we feel most alone, whispering God's promises to our spirit, giving us the courage to take the next step when fear tries to freeze us. They fight battles in the spiritual realm that we never even see, taking on forces of darkness that are gunning for us, but can't get past God's armed guards.

Don't get it twisted, angels are not some passive forces. They're fierce, they're powerful, and they don't back down. When Daniel was praying and fasting for three weeks, an angel showed up and told him, "From the first day you set your heart to understand, your words were heard, and I have come because of your words" (Daniel 10:12 NKJV). But get this; the angel didn't have it easy. He had to fight against demonic resistance, battling the Prince of Persia in the heavenly realms before he could even reach Daniel.

That right there tells you everything you need to know about the lengths angels will go to protect you. They don't mind getting in a fight if it means getting you the help you need. They're out here waging wars you don't even know about, all because you're under God's care, and He's got them on assignment to make sure you're covered.

They're actively involved in every detail of your life, working under God's command to shield you from harm, to deliver you in times of trouble, and to keep you on the path God has set before you.

So the next time you feel surrounded by problems, overwhelmed by trials, or hemmed in by enemies, remember this: you've got heavenly soldiers encamped all around you. They're moving, they're fighting, they're ministering, and they're not backing down. Gods got His angels on duty, and they're working for you, making sure that the hedge is fortified, that you're secure, and that His plans for your life are still on track.

You might not see these angels with your physical eyes, but their impact is all around you. From the moments you narrowly escape disaster to the times you feel a sudden peace wash over you in the middle of chaos, know this: angels are real, they're powerful, and they're part of God's promise to keep you safe. They are a living, breathing part of God's hedge, making sure that no weapon formed against you shall prosper.

So walk with confidence, knowing that you've got backup. God's hedge ismore than just a spiritual concept; it's alive with the presence of His angels, actively working to protect you every step of the way. Stay prayed up, stay faithful, and keep trusting that God's got His first responders on call, ready to move at His command. They're on assignment, and their mission is to keep you covered.

The Power of Prayer

Prayer isn't just something we do out of habit; it's one of the main ways we keep the hedge strong. When we pray, we connect with God, align ourselves with His will, and invite His presence into our situations. Prayer charges up the hedge, activates God's promises, and calls down divine intervention when we need it most.

James 5:16 (NKJV) puts it plainly:

"The effective, fervent prayer of a righteous man avails much."

Your prayers matter. They have power. When you pray, especially when you're in trouble or facing something big, you're reinforcing that hedge, asking God to step in and do what only He can do.

We see this clearly in the story of Daniel. In Daniel 10:12-14 (NKJV), Daniel's prayers set off a spiritual battle in the heavens. An angel was dispatched because of his prayers, showing us that what we do on earth moves things in the spiritual realm. Your prayers are not just words; they're weapons that shape how the hedge operates.

The Role of Faith

Faith is the glue that holds it all together. Without faith, we can't see or trust the hedge around us. Faith lets us rest in God's protection, even when everything around us feels chaotic. It's our faith that tells us, "God's got me, even when I don't see it."

Ephesians 6:16 (NKJV) describes faith as a shield:

"Above all, taking the shield of faith with which you will be able to quench all the fiery darts of the wicked one."

Faith works alongside the hedge, giving it strength. When you trust God and stand firm in your faith, you're reinforcing that protective barrier around you. Faith is not just something you think; it's something you act on. It's choosing to believe God's promises, declaring His Word, and refusing to let fear take control.

Let's not forget, we're in a spiritual battle every day. The enemy is always looking for ways to attack, distract, and discourage us. But God's hedge is our first line of defense, keeping the enemy at bay and giving us the strength to stand our ground.

Paul reminds us in 2 Corinthians 10:4 (NKJV):

"For the weapons of our warfare are not carnal but mighty in God for pulling down strongholds."

We're not fighting with physical weapons; we're fighting with spiritual ones. The hedge is a part of that arsenal, a protective shield that blocks the enemy's attacks. Alongside the hedge, God's Word becomes our sword. When you speak His Word, you're reinforcing that hedge, reminding the enemy that you're under God's protection.

The Influence of Community and Corporate Prayer

It's not just about your personal prayers; community matters too. When believers come together, their collective prayers and faith have an even greater impact on the hedge around them. There's power in unity, and when we pray together, we amplify that protection.

Jesus said in Matthew 18:19-20 (NKJV):

"Again I say to you that if two of you agree on earth concerning anything that they ask, it will be done for them by My Father in heaven. For where two or three are gathered together in My name, I am there in the midst of them."

Corporate prayer creates a powerful force, strengthening the hedge not just around individuals but around entire families, churches, and communities. When we unite in prayer, we're not just standing in the gap; we're building an unbreakable wall of protection.

The Dynamic Nature of the Hedge

One thing to always remember: the hedge isn't fixed. Just like a hedge in the natural realm, it moves, grows, and adapts based on what's going on in our lives and how we're living. When we're drawing closer to God, praying, and walking in obedience, that hedge gets stronger. But if we're neglecting our spiritual life, falling into sin, or drifting away, that hedge can weaken, making us more vulnerable.

But here's the good news: no matter how weak the hedge gets, God is always ready to rebuild it. Through repentance, renewed faith, and a commitment to prayer, we can restore the hedge, making it stronger than ever.

Living Within the Hedge

Knowing how the hedge operates should change the way you live. It's not just about believing in God's protection; it's about actively engaging with it. This means staying committed to prayer, walking in faith, and living in obedience to God's Word. It also means being aware of the spiritual battle we're in and using the weapons God's given us.

1 Peter 5:8-9 (NKJV) gives us this warning:

"Be sober, be vigilant; because your adversary the devil walks about like a roaring lion, seeking whom he may devour. Resist him, steadfast in the

faith, knowing that the same sufferings are experienced by your brother-hood in the world."

We can't afford to be passive. Living within the hedge means staying alert, standing firm, and relying on God's protection daily.

Conclusion: Embracing God's Protective Power

God's hedge of protection is not just a wall; it's a living, breathing shield that works through His sovereignty and love, the activity of angels, the power of prayer, and the strength of our faith. Understanding this helps us appreciate the depth of God's involvement in our lives.

As you continue on this journey of understanding the hedge, let it inspire you to live intentionally within its safety. Stay connected to God, keep your prayer life active, and trust that His hedge is working for you, even when you can't see it.

In the upcoming chapters, we'll dive deeper into practical ways to live within the hedge, how to spot when it's weakened, and what you can do to restore it. We'll also look at how staying within God's boundaries isn't about restriction but about experiencing the fullness of His protection and purpose for your life.

Remember, God's hedge is your shield, His angels are your defenders, and His sovereignty is your assurance. Whatever comes your way, you're not facing it alone; you're surrounded by God's protection, every step of the way.

CHAPTER SIX

LIVING WITHIN THE HEDGE

UNDERSTANDING THE IMPORTANCE OF BOUNDARIES: GOD'S LINES THAT PROTECT AND PROSPER US

A lright, God's hedge aren't just about being covered; it's about respecting the boundaries that God Himself has laid out for our good. These boundaries aren't there to box you in, limit your freedom, or cramp your style. No, these are divine guidelines, set up by the Creator of the universe, to keep you safe, to steer you away from danger, and to guide you straight into the fullness of His blessings. It's like being in a secure fortress where the walls are not there to confine you but to protect you, to preserve what God has placed in you, and to guard the path He's laid out for your life.

They are strong, unshakable, and designed specifically to keep out anything that could harm you. They're not there just to keep you from doing stuff but to keep you within the realm of God's will, purpose, and plan for your life. It's like God saying, "I've set you up for success,

I've put you on a path that leads to life, but you gotta stay within these lines I've drawn."

See, we often think of boundaries as restrictions; something to keep us from what we want; but God's boundaries are designed to keep us aligned with His will. They are like a safety net, making sure that as we navigate life, we're not wandering into areas that will harm us or distract us from what He's called us to be. They keep the enemy's plans at bay and preserve the blessings that God has stored up for you.

David hit the nail on the head when he wrote in Psalm 16:5-6 (NKJV): *"O Lord, You are the portion of my inheritance and my cup; You maintain my lot. The lines have fallen to me in pleasant places; Yes, I have a good inheritance."* David understood something deep here; God's lines, His boundaries, are not a curse; they're a blessing. David's saying, "These lines God has drawn? They're good. They keep me in pleasant places, surrounded by His goodness."

Think about that for a second. Those lines are like guardrails on a mountain road; they're not there to restrict you but to keep you from flying off the edge. They guide you along the path where God's favor flows, where His protection covers, and where His blessings are poured out in abundance. David knew that inside those lines, he was safe, he was blessed, and he was exactly where he needed to be.

These boundaries are not just rules; they're expressions of God's love. They're like a father's wisdom wrapped around you, saying, "I know the way, and I'm leading you in it." When God sets up boundaries,

He's not being restrictive; He's being protective. He's keeping us from the traps, the pitfalls, and the snares that the enemy has set up on the outside. It's God saying, "Stay here where I can bless you, where I can keep you, and where you can hear My voice clearly."

Boundaries aren't about missing out; they're about walking in God's best. They keep us from settling for less when God has more, from stumbling into the darkness when He's called us into the light. When you start to see God's boundaries as His way of securing you, guiding you, and pouring out His goodness on your life, you start embracing them instead of fighting against them.

But the truth is, there are times when we step outside of those boundaries. We get tempted, distracted, or sometimes just plain rebellious. We start thinking that maybe the grass is greener on the other side, or we think we know better than God. But when we step outside the lines, that's when the trouble starts. That's when we open ourselves up to attacks, to unnecessary hardships, and to the consequences that God never intended for us to face.

God's boundaries are like those "Do Not Enter" signs; they're warnings to keep us safe. You gotta recognize when you've wandered too far, when you're playing too close to the edge, and when you've stepped outside the zone of His protection. It's not that God stops loving you; it's that you've stepped outside of the place where His protection flows freely. And the good news is, you can always get back inside those boundaries by repenting, realigning, and running back to where God's grace meets you.

Living within God's hedge means embracing His boundaries. Love them, respect them, and recognize that they're there to lead you into a life of abundance. They're there to keep you connected to God's heart, close to His guidance, and far from the schemes of the enemy. They're not burdens; they're blessings, designed to keep you flourishing in every season of life.

So, keep your eyes on those lines God has drawn. Don't see them as limits but as loving guardrails that keep you on the road to God's best. And remember, inside those lines, you're not just safe; you're blessed, you're protected, and you're living in the fullness of God's plan. Let His boundaries be your place of peace, your strong tower, and your assurance that as long as you stay within the hedge, God's got you c overed.

Obedience is key to staying within the hedge. It's not about just following rules; it's about aligning your heart and actions with what God wants for you. It's saying "yes" to God in your everyday decisions.

Jesus made it clear in John 14:15 (NKJV):

"If you love Me, keep My commandments."

Our obedience shows our love and trust in God. Every time we choose God'sway over our own, we're reinforcing that hedge, making it stronger. This daily commitment keeps us within God's boundaries and under His protection.

The Role of Spiritual Disciplines

Spiritual disciplines like prayer, Bible reading, fasting, and worship are like workout sessions for your soul. They keep you connected to God and sensitive to His leading. When you're disciplined in these practices, you're building up the hedge around you, keeping it strong.

Paul breaks it down in 1 Timothy 4:7-8 (NKJV):

"But reject profane and old wives' fables, and exercise yourself toward godliness. For bodily exercise profits a little, but godliness is profitable for all things, having promise of the life that now is and of that which is to come."

Just like hitting the gym strengthens your body, spiritual disciplines strengthen your relationship with God. They're not about earning points with God; they're about staying in the flow of His guidance and protection.

Recognizing the Signs of a Weakened Hedge

Sometimes the hedge around us can start to weaken, and if we're not careful, we can find ourselves outside of God's protective boundaries without even realizing it. Here are some signs that the hedge may be weakening:

1. **Increased Temptation and Spiritual Attack**: If you're feeling bombarded by temptation or under constant spiritual attack, it might

be a sign that the hedge is thinning. It could be due to unconfessed sin, skipping out on spiritual disciplines, or just drifting away from God.

2.   **Lack of Peace and Assurance**: God's protection brings peace. If you're feeling anxious, fearful, or like something's just not right, it might be a signal that you're stepping outside the hedge. God's peace is a sign you're within His protection; when it's gone, it's time to check in with Him.

3.   **Disobedience and Compromise**: Making choices that go against what you know God wants for you weakens the hedge. When you start compromising your values or living in disobedience, you're stepping outside God's boundaries.

4.   **Diminished Spiritual Hunger**: If you've lost your appetite for prayer, worship, or reading God's Word, that's a warning sign. Spiritual apathy makes you vulnerable, and when you're not engaged with God, you're not staying within the hedge.

Steps to Strengthen and Restore the Hedge

If you sense that the hedge around you is weakening, it's not too late to fix it. God's always ready to welcome you back and restore His protection when you turn to Him. Here's how you can strengthen and restore the hedge:

1.   **Repent and Seek Forgiveness**: If you know sin has caused the hedge to weaken, the first thing to do is repent and ask God for forgiveness. 1 John 1:9 (NKJV) reassures us:

"If we confess our sins, He is faithful and just to forgive us our sins and to cleanse us from all unrighteousness."

Repentance restores our connection to God and invites His grace to rebuild the hedge.

2.   **Recommit to Obedience**: Get back on track by recommitting to obeying God's Word. Reflect on where you've gone off course and make the choice to realign with what God says. Obedience strengthens the hedge and keeps you under God's covering.

3.   **Engage in Spiritual Disciplines**: Dive back into the spiritual disciplines that keep you connected to God. Make time for prayer, reading the Bible, worship, and fasting. These practices are like putting bricks back in the wall of your hedge, reinforcing your protection.

4.   **Seek Accountability and Community**: Don't do this alone. Get around other believers who can encourage you, pray with you, and hold you accountable. Hebrews 10:24-25 (NKJV) reminds us:

"And let us consider one another in order to stir up love and good works, not forsaking the assembling of ourselves together, as is the manner of some, but exhorting one another, and so much the more as you see the Day approaching."

Community keeps you strong, helps you stay focused, and supports you in keeping the hedge intact.

5.   **Pray for God's Protection**: Never under estimate the power of prayer. Regularly ask God to protect you, your family, and your com-

munity. Psalm 91 is a powerful example of how to pray for protection, showing us that staying close to God is key to living under His covering.

Prayer Example: A Prayer for God's Protection

Heavenly Father, we come before You today, lifting up Your mighty name because You are our refuge and fortress, our God in whom we trust (Psalm 91:2). Lord, we thank You that You are a shield around us, our glory, and the One who lifts our head high (Psalm 3:3). We come boldly, seeking Your protection over our lives, our families, and our communities.

Lord, Your Word declares in Psalm 91 that those who dwell in the secret place of the Most High shall abide under the shadow of the Almighty. Father, we come seeking that secret place, that divine shelter where no weapon formed against us shall prosper (Isaiah 54:17). We declare right now that we will make You our dwelling place, for You are our safe haven, our hiding place, and our shield.

Father, Your Word says that You will give Your angels charge over us, to keep us in all our ways (Psalm 91:11). Right now, we pray for those angels to encamp all around us and deliver us from every scheme, every trap, and every plan of the enemy (Psalm 34:7). Lord, let Your angels stand guard over our homes, our families, and our hearts, so that no harm shall come near our dwelling.

We ask, Lord, that You cover us with Your feathers and under Your wings, we will find refuge. Let Your faithfulness be our shield and rampart (Psalm 91:4). Father, we declare that we will not fear the terror of night, nor the arrow that flies by day, because we know that You are our protector, watching over us day and night (Psalm 121:7-8).

God, we pray that You keep us from all evil, that You preserve our going out and our coming in from this time forth, and even forevermore (Psalm 121:8). Surround us, Lord, like mountains around Jerusalem, that no enemy can breach the hedge You have placed around us (Psalm 125:2).

Father, help us to stay close to You, walking in Your will and obeying Your commands, so that Your hedge of protection remains strong around us. Teach us to seek You in all things, to trust You with our whole hearts, and to rely on Your strength alone. Remind us, God, that in You, we find safety, peace, and the fullness of life.

Lord, we declare Psalm 91 over our lives: that You are our refuge, our place of safety; that no evil shall befall us, and no plague shall come near our homes because You are our dwelling place. We speak protection, provision, and peace over every person connected to us, and we trust You, God, to guard our hearts, minds, and lives in Christ Jesus.

In Jesus' mighty name, we pray. Amen.

Living with Vigilance and Awareness

Living within the hedge requires you to stay alert. You've got to be aware of what's happening spiritually and be proactive in keeping yourself within God's protective boundaries. The enemy is always looking for ways to lure you out, so it's crucial to stay vigilant.

1 Peter 5:8 (NKJV) warns us:

"Be sober, be vigilant; because your adversary the devil walks about like a roaring lion, seeking whom he may devour."

Being vigilant means being spiritually awake, recognizing when you're being tempted to step outside God's will, and taking quick action to get back inside the hedge. It's about staying sharp, staying connected to God, and continually working on your spiritual growth.

The Rewards of Living Within the Hedge

When you live within God's hedge, you experience blessings that go beyond physical safety. There's a peace that comes from knowing you're in God's will, a sense of security, and a confidence that no matter what comes your way, you're covered.

Isaiah 26:3 (NKJV) beautifully captures this:

"You will keep him in perfect peace, whose mind is stayed on You, because he trusts in You."

Living within the hedge means living in peace, knowing that God's got you. It's a peace that's deeper than your circumstances because it's rooted in God's presence and promises.

Conclusion

Choosing to live within God's hedge is just that; a choice. It's about being intentional, committed, and vigilant. It's about embracing the boundaries God has set, not as restrictions, but as the place where we find life, protection, and His best for us.

As we continue our journey, let's make the decision to stay within the hedge, honoring God's boundaries and living in a way that keeps us under His protection. By doing this, we'll experience the peace, security, and blessings that come from living under the care of our loving Father.

In the next chapter, we'll explore what happens when we step outside the hedge and the spiritual dangers that lie beyond God's protective boundaries. But for now, rest in knowing that as long as you're within the hedge, you're safe in the arms of the One who loves you and calls you His own.

CHAPTER SEVEN

THE CONSEQUENCES OF STEPPING OUTSIDE THE HEDGE

UNDERSTANDING THE SPIRITUAL RISKS

God's hedge of protection is like a divine barrier, keeping us safe and secure within the boundaries of His will. But let's be real; what happens when we decide to step outside that protection? Sometimes it's a deliberate choice, other times it's a slow drift, but either way, stepping outside the hedge leaves us vulnerable to all kinds of spiritual and physical dangers that can mess up our lives in ways we never imagined. In this chapter, we're going to dive deep into the consequences of stepping outside the hedge, looking at the risks involved, why we choose to leave, and how to get back when we've strayed too far.

This isn't about scaring you; it's about shaking us awake, making us aware so that we stay vigilant and keep ourselves inside the protective boundaries God has set. Let's look at how this plays out, starting from the very beginning.

The Allure of Independence

One of the main reasons folks step outside the hedge is that desire for independence. You know that feeling; the urge to do things your own way, chase after what looks good to you, without checking in with God. It's that pull to be the boss of your own life, and it's an old, familiar story that goes all the way back to Adam and Eve in the Garden of Eden.

When God set up that first hedge around Adam and Eve, He gave them everything they needed, plus one boundary: "Do not eat from the tree of the knowledge of good and evil" (Genesis 2:16-17). But what happened? That slick serpent slid in with his lies, whispering that they could be like God, knowing good and evil for themselves. They wanted independence; they wanted to be in control. So they stepped outside of God's hedge, and immediately, everything changed. The protection lifted, shame and fear entered, and paradise was lost.

Proverbs 16:18 (NKJV) warns us about the dangers of pride:
"Pride goes before destruction, and a haughty spirit before a fall."

Just like Adam and Eve, pride tricks us into thinking we don't need God's protection, that we can handle life on our own terms. It's one of the enemy's oldest tricks, convincing us to step out of the safety of the hedge and into a world of chaos, confusion, and spiritual warfare.

The Prodigal Son: Running Toward the World

Then there's the Prodigal Son, a classic story of stepping outside the hedge (Luke 15:11-32). This young man had everything he needed right in his father's house, but the allure of independence was strong. He thought he knew better; he wanted his inheritance now. So, he took what was his, left the safety of his father's house, and ran straight into a world that promised freedom but delivered nothing but heartache.

The Prodigal Son lived it up for a while, but eventually, he found himself broke, broken, and far from home, feeding pigs just to survive. That's the thing; when you step outside God's hedge, it might look good for a minute, but it won't be long before you realize that you're not where you're supposed to be. The world doesn't care about you like God does; it'll chew you up and spit you out, leaving you empty and desperate.

But here's the beauty of the Prodigal Son's story: even when you've wandered far, God is always waiting, watching, and ready to welcome you back. The moment that young man decided to return, his father ran to meet him, threw his arms around him, and restored him to his rightful place. That's what God wants to do for you. If you've stepped outside the hedge, He's calling you back, ready to restore, renew, and r ebuild.

When we step outside God's hedge, we're not just outside some imaginary boundary; we're stepping out into a battlefield. The Bible makes it clear that we're in a spiritual war, and without God's protection, we're wide open to the enemy's attacks. The devil doesn't fight fair; he's a roaring lion looking for someone to devour (1 Peter 5:8). And when we're outside the hedge, we're his prime target.

This spiritual exposure can show up as sudden temptations, overwhelming doubts, or crises that seem to come out of nowhere. It's not that God's left us; it's that we've walked out from under His covering. When you're not where God has called you to be, you're exposed; plain and simple.

Stepping outside the hedge isn't just about physical risks; it's about the spiritual fallout that comes with disobedience. We've seen it with Israel over and over again. God would set them up with protection, blessings, and favor, but when they turned away, chasing idols and doing their own thing, God would lower that hedge and let them face the consequences.

It's not that God doesn't want to protect us; it's that our choices matter. Just like Adam and Eve, the Prodigal Son, and the Israelites, we have a say in whether we live inside the hedge or not. It's up to us to choose God's way, to stay within His boundaries, and to recognize that His rules are there for our good, not to hold us back.

Finding Your Way Back

If you've found yourself outside the hedge, don't lose hope. Remember, God is always ready to restore. Just like the Prodigal Son, all it takes is a turn; a decision to come back to God. He's not waiting with condemnation; He's waiting with open arms, ready to wrap you up in His protection once again.

Repent, realign, and run back to the safety of God's hedge. There's no shame in admitting you've wandered. There's only grace, forgiveness, and the promise of renewed protection when you come back home.

So, take that step today. Don't wait. God's hedge is not just a line of defense; it's His loving arms, ready to surround you, keep you safe, and guide you in every step.

The Reality of Spiritual Exposure

When we step outside of God's hedge of protection, we leave ourselves wide open to spiritual attack. We're not just talking about a minor setback; we're talking about being exposed in a spiritual war zone. The Bible doesn't mince words; Satan is always on the hunt, prowling like a lion, hungry to tear us apart. Without God's hedge, we become easy targets, vulnerable to every lie, temptation, and scheme the enemy throws our way. And believe me, he's not playing games; he's out for blood.

1 Peter 5:8 (NKJV) lays it all out:
"Be sober, be vigilant; because your adversary the devil walks about like a roaring lion, seeking whom he may devour."

Outside the hedge, we're like sitting ducks. The shield we once took for granted is gone, and we're left trying to fend off attacks on our own strength; weak, tired, and overwhelmed. This spiritual exposure shows up in so many ways: you feel constantly under pressure, like the walls are closing in, temptations seem harder to resist, and there's this spiritual fog that clouds your mind, leaving you confused, lost, and doubting everything you thought you knew. That's what happens when we're out here without God's protection; we're vulnerable, and the enemy knows it.

The Consequence of Disobedience

Disobedience to God's commands is like a one-way ticket straight out of the hedge. The Bible is packed with stories of individuals and whole nations who thought they could do things their way, ignoring God's clear instructions. And what happened? They lost the protection God had graciously put around them.

One of the most glaring examples is King Saul. God handpicked Saul to be Israel's first king. He had the anointing, the blessing, and God's favor. But Saul couldn't stay obedient; he kept doing things his own way, cutting corners, and ignoring God's direct orders. That disobedience cost him dearly. God took away His protection, and Saul's life spiraled out of control.

The prophet Samuel put it plainly in 1 Samuel 15:22-23 (NKJV):
"Has the Lord as great delight in burnt offerings and sacrifices, as in obeying the voice of the Lord? Behold, to obey is better than sacrifice, and to heed than the fat of rams. For rebellion is as the sin of witchcraft, and stubbornness is as iniquity and idolatry. Because you have rejected the word of the Lord, He also has rejected you from being king."

Saul's disobedience didn't just lose him his crown; it cost him his peace, his purpose, and God's protective covering. He was left exposed, vulnerable, and ultimately, destroyed. Saul's downfall is a hard reminder:

disobedience doesn't just disappoint God; it opens us up to dangers we're not equipped to handle.

The Consequence of Sin

Sin is like an open wound that invites infection. When we let sin run unchecked in our lives, it creates a chasm between us and God, weakening the hedge that's supposed to keep us safe. Sin doesn't just damage our relationship with God; it leaves us defenseless against the enemy. Whether it's pride, lying, greed, or any other sin, it all has the same effect; it distances us from God and strips away His protection.

Isaiah 59:1-2 (NKJV) makes it crystal clear:
"Behold, the Lord's hand is not shortened, that it cannot save; nor His ear heavy, that it cannot hear. But your iniquities have separated you from your God; and your sins have hidden His face from you, so that He will not hear."

God's power hasn't changed, and His ears aren't closed, but our sins are blocking the line of communication. It's not that He doesn't want to protect us; it's that our sin has us out of bounds. And trust, the impact of sin is real. You feel it in your relationships breaking down, the constant inner turmoil, the guilt, and sometimes, it even manifests physically. Sin weakens us spiritually, and once that hedge is compromised, the enemy moves in quick. That's why repentance is critical; it's the only way to patch that breach and get back inside God's protective c overing.

The Consequence of Neglect

Sometimes, it's not outright disobedience or blatant sin that gets us outside the hedge; it's neglect. It's that slow drift when we stop praying like we used to, when the Bible starts collecting dust, and we skip church more often than not. It's not always a deliberate rebellion; sometimes it's just life creeping in and taking over. But spiritual neglect is dangerous; it's like a slow leak in your tire; you don't notice it until you're stranded on the side of the road.

Hebrews 2:1 (NKJV) warns us against this kind of drift:
"Therefore we must give the more earnest heed to the things we have heard, lest we drift away."

Neglect might not feel like outright rebellion, but it's just as deadly. The enemy loves when we let our guard down, when we're too busy, too tired, or too distracted to stay connected to God. Before we know it, we're outside the hedge, fighting battles we were never meant to fight on our own. Neglect is subtle, but its consequences are serious; leaving us weak, spiritually malnourished, and exposed to attacks we don't see com ing.

Wrapping It Up

Whether it's disobedience, sin, or just plain neglect, stepping outside of God's hedge leaves us wide open to attack. But God, in His mercy, always makes a way back. It starts with recognizing where you are, repenting, and running back to the One who never stopped wanting to protect you. God's hedge is there for a reason; it's not just to keep you safe; it's to keep you close. Don't take it for granted; stay within His boundaries, because outside the hedge, there's nothing but trouble w aiting.

Recognizing When You've Stepped Outside the Hedge

It's important to recognize when you've stepped outside the hedge so you can get back in. Here are some signs that you may have wandered out of God's protection:

1. **Feeling Distant from God**: If you're feeling disconnected from God, it might be because you've moved away from His protective presence.

2. **Increased Spiritual Warfare**: If you're experiencing heightened attacks, temptations, or confusion, it's a sign you might be outside the hedge and more vulnerable to the enemy.

3. **Lack of Peace**: Constant anxiety, fear, or a lack of peace can signal that you've stepped outside the boundaries God set to keep you safe.

4. **Conviction of Sin**: If you're feeling convicted about certain behaviors, that's God's way of letting you know it's time to repent and return.

5. **Spiritual Apathy**: Losing your hunger for prayer, worship, or the Word can indicate that you've drifted away from God's protection.

Returning to the Safety of the Hedge

If you recognize that you've stepped outside the hedge, it's not too late to come back. Here's how you can return to God's protection:

1.   **Repentance**: Start by repenting and asking God for forgiveness. Repentance isn't just about feeling bad; it's about turning away from what led you astray and turning back to God.

Acts 3:19 (NKJV) encourages us:

"Repent therefore and be converted, that your sins may be blotted out, so that times of refreshing may come from the presence of the Lord."

Repentance brings restoration and refreshment, pulling us back into the safety of God's hedge.

2.   **Renew Your Commitment to Obedience**: Decide to get back in line with God's Word. Obedience invites God's protection and rebuilds the hedge around your life.

3.   **Reengage in Spiritual Disciplines**: Get back into your spiritual habits; prayer, Bible reading, worship. These disciplines reconnect you with God and strengthen the hedge.

4.   **Seek Accountability**: Find other believers who can encourage you, hold you accountable, and help you stay on track. Being part of a community can keep you within the hedge.

5.   **Pray for Restoration**: Ask God to restore His protection over your life. Psalm 51:12 (NKJV) captures this prayer beautifully:

"Restore to me the joy of Your salvation, and uphold me by Your generous Spirit."

Prayer can mend the breaks in the hedge, inviting God's protection back into your life.

Living with a Renewed Awareness: A High Cost You Can't Afford to Pay

Once you find your way back into God's hedge, you gotta live with your eyes wide open. This isn't the time to get comfortable or sloppy. That renewed awareness of what it cost you when you stepped out should keep you on your toes. Paul puts it plainly in *Ephesians 5:15-16; walk like you got some sense, because these days are full of traps.* Walking wisely means you're staying sharp, watching your back, keeping up with your prayer life, reading the Word, and leaning on God's guidance like never before.

The cost of stepping outside that hedge? It's high, real high. Pride, disobedience, sin, neglect, each one can mess you up spiritually, emotionally, and even physically. But here's the good news: no matter how far you've gone, God's grace is right there, reaching out to pull you back. Repent, obey, and recommit. Learn from every misstep, recognize the enemy's schemes, and make staying within God's boundaries your top p riority.

Bottom line: stepping outside the hedge isn't worth it. The safest, most blessed place you can ever be is right in the protective care of a God who loves you fiercely. Don't take that for granted. Guard it, cherish it, and live every day soaked in the peace, security, and abundance that only come from being covered by His mighty hand.

CHAPTER EIGHT

MAINTAINING A STRONG HEDGE

THE IMPORTANCE OF SPIRITUAL VIGILANCE

Now that we've talked about what happens when you step outside the hedge of God's protection, let's focus on how to keep that hedge strong and unbreakable in your life. Maintaining the hedge isn't just a one-time thing; it's an ongoing process that requires effort, intentionality, and a constant watchfulness over your spiritual life.

You've got to nurture your relationship with God, stay in line with His will, and be on guard against anything that might weaken the protection He's placed around you. In this chapter, we'll dive into practical ways to keep your hedge strong, the role of spiritual disciplines, the importance of community, and how to recognize and fix any breaches that might come up in your spiritual protection.

The Foundation: A Life Built on God's Word

The strongest hedge starts with a life built on God's Word. Jesus made this clear in the parable of the wise and foolish builders. In Matthew 7:24-25(NKJV), He says:

"Therefore whoever hears these sayings of Mine, and does them, I will liken him to a wise man who built his house on the rock: and the rain descended, the floods came, and the winds blew and beat on that house; and it did not fall, for it was founded on the rock."

Building your life on God's Word isn't just about reading the Bible; it's about living it out every day. It means letting Scripture shape how you think, how you act, and how you make decisions. When your life is grounded in God's truth, you're setting up a hedge that can withstand whatever storms life throws at you.

We've talked about how prayer is a powerful tool for maintaining a strong hedge. It's through prayer that we stay connected to God, seek His guidance, and call on His protection. Prayer isn't just about asking God to keep you safe; it's about building a relationship where you're constantly inviting God into every part of your life.

Philippians 4:6-7 (NKJV) encourages us:

"Be anxious for nothing, but in everything by prayer and supplication, with thanksgiving, let your requests be made known to God; and the peace of God, which surpasses all understanding, will guard your hearts and minds through Christ Jesus."

Prayer keeps your heart and mind under God's watchful care. It's a way of saying, "God, I trust You with my life." When you pray consistently, you're not just talking to God—you're strengthening the hedge that surrounds you.

Spiritual disciplines like fasting, worship, meditating on Scripture, and participating in sacraments like communion are vital in keeping your hedge strong. These practices help you grow in your faith, sharpen your spiritual senses, and reinforce your commitment to stay within God's protective boundaries.

Paul gives this advice in 1 Timothy 4:7-8 (NKJV):

"But reject profane and old wives' fables, and exercise yourself toward godliness. For bodily exercise profits a little, but godliness is profitable for all things, having promise of the life that now is and of that which is to come."

Just like working out keeps your body fit, spiritual disciplines keep your spirit strong. They're not just routines; they're ways to connect more deeply with God, building up the hedge that keeps you protected.

The Importance of Accountability and Community

A strong hedge is often supported by the people around you. Having accountability partners, mentors, and a church community can help you stay on the right path. They provide guidance, encouragement, and correction when you need it most.

Ecclesiastes 4:9-10 (NKJV) reminds us:

"Two are better than one, because they have a good reward for their labor. For if they fall, one will lift up his companion. But woe to him who is alone when he falls, for he has no one to help him up."

When you surround yourself with other believers who share your commitment to God, you strengthen your hedge. These relationships keep you accountable, offer wisdom, and help you stay firm in your walk with God.

Recognizing and Addressing Breaches in the Hedge

Even when you're doing your best, there might be times when the hedge around you gets weak or breached. It's crucial to spot these breaches early and take action to repair them before they cause further damage.

Here are some signs that your hedge might be compromised:

1.   **Increased Temptation and Spiritual Attack**: If you notice more frequent or intense spiritual attacks, it could be a sign that your hedge is weakened. This might happen because of unconfessed sin, neglecting your spiritual disciplines, or drifting away from God.

2.   **Diminished Peace and Assurance**: Losing your sense of peace or feeling insecure might mean your hedge is compromised. God's protection brings peace; if it's missing, it's time to check where you stand spiritually.

3. **Compromised Integrity or Disobedience**: If you find yourself compromising your values or living in disobedience to God, that weakens the hedge. It's essential to recognize this, repent, and get back in line with God's will.

When you identify a breach, here's how to address it:

1. **Confession and Repentance**: Start by confessing any sin that might have caused the breach and repent. 1 John 1:9 (NKJV) assures us:

"If we confess our sins, He is faithful and just to forgive us our sins and to cleanse us from all unrighteousness."

Confession and repentance restore your relationship with God and help rebuild your hedge.

2. **Renewed Commitment to Spiritual Disciplines**: Strengthen your commitment to prayer, Bible study, worship, and other spiritual practices. These will help you reconnect with God and reinforce the hedge around you.

3. **Seek Godly Counsel and Accountability**: If you're struggling to fix the hedge on your own, don't hesitate to seek help from a trusted mentor, pastor, or accountability partner. They can provide the support and guidance you need.

4. **Pray for God's Restoration**: Ask God to restore His protection over your life. David's prayer in Psalm 51:10-12 (NKJV) is a powerful example:

"Create in me a clean heart, O God, and renew a steadfast spirit within me. Do not cast me away from Your presence, and do not take Your Holy Spirit from me. Restore to me the joy of Your salvation, and uphold me by Your generous Spirit."

God is always ready to restore and strengthen your hedge when you come to Him with a sincere heart.

Living in the Power of the Holy Spirit

One of the best ways to keep your hedge strong is to live by the power of the Holy Spirit. The Holy Spirit is your guide, comforter, and protector, equipping you to live in line with God's will and stand strong against the enemy's attacks.

Paul reminds us in Galatians 5:16 (NKJV):

"I say then: Walk in the Spirit, and you shall not fulfill the lust of the flesh."

Walking in the Spirit means letting the Holy Spirit lead every part of your life. It's about daily surrender, listening to His guidance, and relying on His strength. When you live in the Spirit, you're empowered to keep your hedge intact and stay within God's will.

In the next chapters, we'll explore how to help others find their way back to God's protection and how to live a life that continually invites His presence and guidance. But for now, commit yourself to maintaining a strong hedge, knowing it's the key to experiencing God's peace, security, and blessings under His watchful care.

Let this understanding of maintaining the hedge encourage you to guard your spiritual life with everything you've got. Keep pressing into God, stay connected to His Word, and rely on the power of the Holy Spirit to protect and guide you. In doing so, you'll live securely within the hedge of His protection, experiencing the fullness of His love and grace every day.

CHAPTER NINE

HELPING OTHERS FIND THEIR WAY BACK TO THE HEDGE

THE CALL TO SPIRITUAL RESTORATION

As followers of Christ, our responsibility doesn't end with our own spiritual well-being. We're also called to look out for others, especially those who have wandered away from God's protection. When we see someone stepping outside the hedge, whether it's because of sin, neglect, or just plain old disobedience, it's our job to help guide them back to safety. This chapter is all about how we can fulfill that calling, offering some real talk on how to approach, support, and restore those who've strayed.

Understanding the Ministry of Reconciliation

The Bible makes it clear: we're called to be agents of reconciliation, helping to restore those who've fallen away from God. Paul breaks it down in 2 Corinthians 5:18-20 (NKJV):

"Now all things are of God, who has reconciled us to Himself through Jesus Christ, and has given us the ministry of reconciliation, that is, that God was in Christ reconciling the world to Himself, not imputing their trespasses to them, and has committed to us the word of reconciliation. Now then, we are ambassadors for Christ, as though God were pleading through us: we implore you on Christ's behalf, be reconciled to God."

We are ambassadors for Christ, y'all. That means we've got a mission, to help others get back to God. It's a big part of what we're called to do as believers. And it requires us to approach those who've stepped away with compassion, patience, and a whole lot of love.

Approaching with Love and Compassion

When you see someone outside the hedge, don't come at them with judgment or condemnation. Instead, approach them with love and compassion. Galatians 6:1 (NKJV) lays it out like this:

"Brethren, if a man is overtaken in any trespass, you who are spiritual restore such a one in a spirit of gentleness, considering yourself lest you also be tempted."

Restoration has to be done gently, with a humble heart. None of us are immune to temptation, and we all know what it's like to fall short. Coming at someone with empathy and humility opens the door for true healing and restoration.

Listening and Understanding

Before you start preaching or giving advice, just listen. Sometimes folks just need someone to hear them out. Understanding what's going on in their lives; the struggles, the fears, the reasons why they stepped outside the hedge; is crucial. Listening shows that you care and are genuinely invested in helping them find their way back to God.

James 1:19 (NKJV) gives us wise advice on this:

"So then, my beloved brethren, let every man be swift to hear, slow to speak, slow to wrath."

Taking time to listen creates a safe space for the person to open up, which is often the first step toward healing and coming back to God.

Offering Biblical Guidance

After you've listened and understood their situation, then you can offer some biblical guidance. This might mean pointing them to Scriptures, encouraging repentance, or helping them see where they've veered off course. The key is to do this with love and sensitivity, always rooting your guidance in God's Word.

Paul emphasizes the power of Scripture in 2 Timothy 3:16-17 (NKJV):

"All Scripture is given by inspiration of God, and is profitable for doctrine, for reproof, for correction, for instruction in righteousness, that the man of God may be complete, thoroughly equipped for every good work."

God's Word is a tool for correction and instruction. By sharing Scripture, we help guide others back to the right path and into the safety of God's hedge.

Praying for Restoration

Prayer has to be a part of the process. As you're helping someone find their way back, be sure to pray for them. Ask God to soften their heart, open their eyes, and lead them back to His protection. Prayer invites God into the situation and makes sure you're relying on His power, not your own, to bring about change.

James 5:16 (NKJV) reminds us:

"Confess your trespasses to one another, and pray for one another, that you may be healed. The effective, fervent prayer of a righteous man avails much."

Praying for those who have strayed isn't just something nice to do; it's a powerful act of love and intercession, asking God to step in and bring them back.

Providing Ongoing Support and Accountability

Helping someone get back inside the hedge isn't a one-and-done kind of thing. They'll need ongoing support and accountability. Once they've recognized the need to return to God's protection, stick with them. Encourage them, hold them accountable, and pray with them.

This support is what helps them stay on the right path and strengthens their commitment to live within God's will.

Hebrews 10:24-25 (NKJV) highlights the importance of this kind of support:

"And let us consider one another in order to stir up love and good works, not forsaking the assembling of ourselves together, as is the manner of some, but exhorting one another, and so much the more as you see the Day approaching."

Supporting each other in this walk of faith is a vital part of staying protected. By offering ongoing encouragement, we help each other keep the hedge strong.

One of the most powerful ways to lead someone back to the hedge is simply by living as an example. When people see the peace, security, and blessings that come from living within God's protective boundaries, they'll want that for themselves. Your life can be a light that shows others the beauty of staying in God's will.

Jesus said it best in Matthew 5:16 (NKJV):

"Let your light so shine before men, that they may see your good works and glorify your Father in heaven."

Living in a way that reflects God's goodness isn't just for us; it's a testimony to others, drawing them toward the same protection and joy we experience.

The Joy of Restoration

There's nothing like the joy of seeing someone come back to God. When a fellow believer returns to the safety of the hedge, it's a reason to celebrate. And it's not just us who celebrate; heaven rejoices, too. Jesus shared this joy in the parable of the lost sheep:

Luke 15:7 (NKJV) captures it beautifully:

"I say to you that likewise there will be more joy in heaven over one sinner who repents than over ninety-nine just persons who need no repentance."

The joy of restoration reflects God's heart. He doesn't want anyone to be lost; He wants everyone to come back to Him. When we help someone find their way back, we're sharing in that joy.

Conclusion: A Lifelong Commitment to Reconciliation

Helping others return to God's hedge of protection is a lifelong mission. It takes patience, compassion, and a whole lot of leaning on God's grace and wisdom. As we work to restore those who have strayed, we must do so with humility, always aware of our own need for God's protection and guidance.

In the next chapters, we'll talk about how to live a life that always invites God's presence and keeps us within His protective hedge. But for now, let's commit ourselves to the ministry of reconciliation. Let's be those ambassadors for Christ, helping others find the peace, security, and joy that come from living inside the boundaries God has set.

As we continue this journey, remember that our calling isn't just about our own walk; it's about lifting up our brothers and sisters, bringing them back when they've wandered, and showing them the way back to God's protective care. Together, we can help others experience the fullness of living within the hedge of God's love and grace.

CHAPTER TEN

LIVING A LIFE THAT INVITES GOD'S PRESENCE

THE POWER OF GOD'S PRESENCE: KEEP HIM CLOSE, KEEP THE HEDGE STRONG

As we wrap up our journey through God's hedge of protection, let's bring it home to what really matters: living a life that invites and keeps God's presence close. You gotta understand, the hedge isn't just some invisible barrier keeping danger out; it's all about your connection with God. His presence is the heartbeat of the hedge; it's what keeps it strong, securing your steps, guiding your path, and showering you with blessings that overflow.

In this next chapter, we're digging deep into how to live a life that constantly welcomes God's presence. We'll unpack the power of worship and thanksgiving, explore what it means to truly surrender your heart, and show you how to walk with a keen awareness that God's got you; every moment of every day.

Cultivating a Lifestyle of Worship and Thanksgiving

Worship and thanksgiving are like God's personal invitation to show up and stay. It's not just about singing songs on a Sunday morning; it's about honoring God in every move you make, every word you speak, every thought you think. And thanksgiving? That's the language of a grateful heart that's always acknowledging God's goodness; whether it's the little blessings or the big miracles. When you mix worship and thanksgiving, you create an environment that's irresistible to God. And when God's in the room, so is His peace, His guidance, and His protection.

Psalm 100:4 (NKJV) says it like this:

"Enter into His gates with thanksgiving, and into His courts with praise. Be thankful to Him, and bless His name."

You see, when you live a life of worship and gratitude, you're not just keeping the hedge strong; you're creating a space where God feels welcome. And when God's presence settles in, it changes the whole atmosphere. It's like living under a constant covering where peace replaces anxiety, joy kicks out sorrow, and security silences fear.

Example: King Jehoshaphat and the Power of Praise

Remember King Jehoshaphat? He was faced with a massive army coming against him; way more than he and his people could handle. But instead of panicking or trying to fight in his own strength, Jehoshaphat called the people to worship. They sang praises, thanked God in advance for the victory, and just like that, God showed up and turned the enemy against themselves (2 Chronicles 20:21-22). The battle was won through praise! That's the power of worship and thanksgiving; it invites God to step in and fight for you.

The Surrendered Heart: Letting Go and Letting God

Living in God's presence also requires a surrendered heart. This ain't just about giving up control; it's about laying down your own plans, your ego, your fears, and saying, "God, have Your way." Surrender means trusting that God's way is always better, even when you don't understand what He's doing. It's allowing Him to be Lord over every part of your life; your thoughts, your dreams, your struggles, your t riumphs.

Paul breaks it down in Romans 12:1-2 (NKJV):

"I beseech you therefore, brethren, by the mercies of God, that you present your bodies a living sacrifice, holy, acceptable to God, which is your reasonable service. And do not be conformed to this world, but be transformed by the renewing of your mind, that you may prove what is that good and acceptable and perfect will of God."

A surrendered heart isn't just going through the motions; it's sold out to God, fully committed to His purpose, and open to His direction. When you let God lead, you're putting yourself smack dab in the center of His protection. His presence becomes your guide, your guard, and your greatest comfort.

Example: The Ultimate Surrender – Jesus in Gethsemane

Look at Jesus in the Garden of Gethsemane. He was facing the cross, the most intense trial of His life, and He prayed, *"Not My will, but Yours be done"* (Luke 22:42). That's surrender. He didn't lean on His own understanding or shrink back because of the pain ahead. He trusted the Father's plan completely. And because of that surrender, we now have access to the hedge of salvation and eternal protection. Jesus modeled what it looks like to live fully surrendered, and it's a call for us to do the same.

Living a life that invites God's presence isn't about perfection; it's about positioning. It's about putting God first, trusting Him with everything, and letting His presence fill every corner of your life. So, stay surrendered, keep worshiping, and watch as God's presence surrounds you like a mighty hedge that nothing can break through.

Walking in Obedience

Obedience isn't just about following a bunch of rules; it's about aligning your life with God's Word and responding to His guidance. When you walk in obedience, you show that you trust God and want to stay within the hedge He's put around you.

Jesus ties obedience directly to God's presence in John 14:23 (NKJV):

"Jesus answered and said to him, 'If anyone loves Me, he will keep My word; and My Father will love him, and We will come to him and make Our home with him.'"

Obedience invites God to dwell with you, bringing His presence and protection. It keeps you within the hedge, shielded from whatever the enemy tries to throw at you.

Inviting God's presence means being aware of Him in every moment. Whether you're at work, at home, or just going about your day, it's about knowing God is right there with you. This awareness helps you seek His guidance, lean on His strength, and avoid actions that would pull you away from Him.

Proverbs 3:5-6 (NKJV) encourages us to keep God at the center:

"Trust in the Lord with all your heart, and lean not on your own understanding; in all your ways acknowledge Him, and He shall direct your paths."

Acknowledging God in all you do means you're inviting Him into every detail of your life. This keeps you within His hedge because you're constantly looking to Him for direction and protection.

The Role of Faith and Trust

Faith and trust are foundational when it comes to inviting and maintaining God's presence. Faith is believing in what you can't see, and trust is being confident that God is exactly who He says He is and will do exactly what He's promised.

Psalm 91:2 (NKJV) shows us how trust brings God's protection:

"I will say of the Lord, 'He is my refuge and my fortress; My God, in Him I will trust.'"

When you put your trust in God, you're saying you depend on Him and need His presence. Faith and trust keep you anchored inside the hedge, no matter how tough life gets.

Inviting God's Presence Through Repentance and Purity

Keeping a strong hedge also means committing to purity and holiness. Sin creates distance between us and God, weakening the hedge. Regular self-checks and repentance are key to staying close to God and keeping His presence strong in your life.

James 4:8 (NKJV) calls us to get right with God:

"Draw near to God and He will draw near to you. Cleanse your hands, you sinners; and purify your hearts, you double-minded."

Repentance clears the way for God to be close to you again, making sure the hedge stays solid and your connection to God remains strong.

The Importance of Spiritual Discernment

Living within God's hedge means developing spiritual discernment; the ability to hear God's voice, see what's right and wrong, and recognize the enemy's tricks. Discernment helps you navigate life wisely, making decisions that align with God's will.

1 John 4:1 (NKJV) reminds us:

"Beloved, do not believe every spirit, but test the spirits, whether they are of God; because many false prophets have gone out into the world."

Discernment keeps you from being deceived and helps you stay within the hedge by making choices that are rooted in God's truth.

Living in the Light of Eternity

Finally, living a life that invites God's presence means keeping your eyes on eternity. The hedge isn't just about protection here on earth; it's about preparing us for an eternal life with God. When you live with an eternal perspective, you'll prioritize your relationship with God and make choices that reflect where you're headed.

Paul puts it like this in Colossians 3:2-4 (NKJV):

"Set your mind on things above, not on things on the earth. For you died, and your life is hidden with Christ in God. When Christ who is our life appears, then you also will appear with Him in glory."

Living with eternity in mind helps you focus on what's truly important; your relationship with God. This perspective keeps you committed to staying within the hedge and living a life that continually invites God's presence.

Conclusion: A Life Fully Surrendered to God

Living within God's hedge of protection is about so much more than just seeking safety. It's about a deep relationship with God; a life fully surrendered, obedient, and aware of His presence. When you make God the center of your life, His presence surrounds you, guides you, protects you, and blesses you in ways you never thought possible.

Remember, the hedge isn't just some invisible wall; it's a spiritual reality that reflects your connection to God. Let this book be a reminder that the safest, most secure place you can ever be is within God's hedge, living in His presence, and walking in His will.

Commit to living a life that always invites God's presence. Trust that He is your refuge, your fortress, and your constant help. And as you stay within His hedge, may you experience the peace, joy, and security that come from being under the care of a loving and sovereign God, now and forever.

CHAPTER ELEVEN

GUARDING THE HEDGE IN TIMES OF CRISIS

THE REALITY OF SPIRITUAL WARFARE

W alking with God isn't always smooth sailing. There are seasons when the enemy cranks up his attacks, especially when you're going through a crisis or making serious spiritual progress. These are the times when the hedge of protection around you is crucial, and guarding it becomes your top priority. In this chapter, we're going to break down how to keep your hedge strong during tough times, understand the role of spiritual warfare, and stand firm when the enemy is trying to break through.

Recognizing Spiritual Attacks: Stay Woke, Don't Get Caught Slippin'

The first thing you gotta do to guard your hedge when everything's coming at you is to recognize when you're under spiritual attack. Don't get it twisted; every bad day isn't just a bad day, and every struggle isn't just coincidence. The enemy is slick, and he'll hit you where it hurts; your health, your relationships, your money, your emotions; anything to mess with your mind and shake your faith. His goal? To get you so caught up in the chaos that you step outside of God's protection and forget who's really in control.

The Enemy's Game Plan

The Bible gives us a heads-up about how the enemy moves. In 1 Peter 5:8 (NKJV), it lays it all out:

"Be sober, be vigilant; because your adversary the devil walks about like a roaring lion, seeking whom he may devour."

The devil's on the prowl, y'all. He's always looking for someone who's slipping, someone he can pounce on. And if you're not paying attention, he'll catch you off guard. Spiritual attacks are real, and they can show up in all kinds of ways: sudden sickness, unexpected financial strain, family drama that just won't quit, or even a sense of hopelessness that hits you out of nowhere. It's like the enemy has a playbook, and he's using every trick to get you outside that hedge.

Example: Job—Blindsided by Trials

Take Job, for instance. Job was living his best life; he had money, family, good health, everything was going right. But all of a sudden, everything went left. Out of nowhere, he lost his wealth, his kids, and even his health. Job was blindsided by an attack that hit him from all angles, and it wasn't just by chance. Satan went straight for Job, trying to break him, trying to prove that without all the blessings, Job would fold.

But here's the thing; Job recognized that this wasn't just a string of bad luck; it was a spiritual attack. Even though he was hurt, confused, and struggling, he didn't curse God or turn away. Instead, he stayed in the fight, kept talking to God, and held onto his faith. Job's story shows us that the enemy doesn't play fair, but it also shows that if you keep your eyes on God, you can make it through any attack.

Example: Jesus in the Wilderness—Tempted at His Weakest

Let's not forget Jesus in the wilderness. After fasting for 40 days and nights, Jesus was physically weak; hungry, tired, and vulnerable. And that's exactly when the devil rolled up on Him, trying to tempt Him with everything from food to power. Satan wanted to catch Jesus off guard, to get Him to step outside His purpose.

But Jesus wasn't fooled. He recognized the attack for what it was; a desperate attempt by the enemy to throw Him off His mission. Jesus hit back with the Word of God, saying, "It is written..." (Matthew 4:4). He didn't argue, didn't negotiate; He stood firm and fought back with Scripture. That's how you recognize and shut down a spiritual attack; by staying grounded in God's Word and knowing who you are and whose you are.

Example: Nehemiah—Distractions and Discouragement

Look at Nehemiah when he was rebuilding the wall of Jerusalem. He was right in the middle of doing God's work, but his enemies kept trying to distract and discourage him. They sent threats, spread lies, and even tried to lure him into traps. Nehemiah recognized that all of it was an attempt to stop what God was doing through him.

Instead of letting the enemy get to him, Nehemiah prayed, "Now therefore, O God, strengthen my hands" (Nehemiah 6:9 NKJV). He kept working, kept praying, and kept his eyes on God. Nehemiah knew that the enemy was trying to attack his purpose, but he wasn't about to let that stop him.

The Real Deal: Keep Your Spiritual Eyes Open

When you're under attack, it's easy to feel overwhelmed, like everything is falling apart. But the key is to keep your spiritual eyes open. Know when the enemy is trying to get you off your game. Stay woke, stay prayed up, and keep God's Word close. Recognize the attacks for what they are; attempts to break you and pull you out of God's covering.

So, when life hits hard and you feel surrounded, remember: this isn't just life coming at you. It's a spiritual battle. But God's got your back, and His hedge is still there; strong, protective, and unbreakable as long as you stay connected to Him. Don't let the enemy trick you into thinking you're alone or unprotected. Keep your head up, stay vigilant, and know that God's got the victory lined up for you on the other side of the fight.

Equipping Yourself with the Armor of God

When you're facing spiritual warfare, you've got to suit up with the full armor of God. This armor isn't just for show; it protects you from the enemy's tricks and helps keep your hedge strong.

Paul lays it out in Ephesians 6:13-17 (NKJV):

"Therefore take up the whole armor of God, that you may be able to withstand in the evil day, and having done all, to stand. Stand therefore, having girded your waist with truth, having put on the breastplate of righteousness, and having shod your feet with the preparation of the gospel of peace; above all, taking the shield of faith with which you will be able to quench all the fiery darts of the wicked one. And take the helmet of salvation, and the sword of the Spirit, which is the word of God."

Each piece of this armor has a purpose: truth keeps you grounded, righteousness guards your heart, peace steadies your steps, faith blocks the enemy's attacks, salvation covers your mind, and God's Word is your weapon. Putting on this armor daily is like locking the gate around your hedge; keeping it secure no matter what comes at you.

Standing Firm in Faith

When you're in the thick of a crisis, standing firm in your faith is everything. Faith isn't just about believing God exists; it's about trusting in who He is, His promises, and His power to protect you. Faith keeps you inside the hedge when everything else is trying to pull you out.

Hebrews 11:6 (NKJV) reminds us how crucial faith is:

"But without faith it is impossible to please Him, for he who comes to God must believe that He is, and that He is a rewarder of those who diligently seek Him."

Faith isn't passive; it's active. It's the kind of trust that makes you keep seeking God, especially when times are hard. Your faith is what keeps you standing, knowing that God's got your back, even when the battle is fierce.

The Power of Prayer and Fasting

Prayer and fasting are powerhouse tools for guarding your hedge during a crisis. Prayer connects you directly to God, asking Him to step in and take control. Fasting, on the other hand, sharpens your focus on God, cutting out distractions and showing your dependence on Him.

Jesus teaches about the impact of prayer and fasting in Matthew 17:21 (NKJV):

"However, this kind does not go out except by prayer and fasting."

When you combine prayer with fasting, you're turning up the heat on the enemy and reinforcing your hedge. It shows God you're serious and fully leaning on Him to bring you through whatever you're facing.

In any crisis, remember that the battle is the Lord's. Yes, you've got to stand firm and do your part, but it's God's strength that holds it all together. You're not out here fighting alone; God's got this.

The prophet Jahaziel told King Jehoshaphat and the people of Judah the same thing in 2 Chronicles 20:15 (NKJV):

"Thus says the Lord to you: 'Do not be afraid nor dismayed because of this great multitude, for the battle is not yours, but God's.'"

When you lean on God's strength, you can face whatever crisis comes your way with confidence, knowing that He's the one fighting for you and keeping your hedge intact.

Don't try to handle crises on your own. Lean into your community of believers. Their prayers, encouragement, and wisdom can help reinforce your hedge when you feel weak.

James 5:16 (NKJV) emphasizes the power of collective prayer:

"Confess your trespasses to one another, and pray for one another, that you may be healed. The effective, fervent prayer of a righteous man avails much."

By surrounding yourself with fellow believers, you're not just getting support; you're adding layers to your hedge. Each person's faith and prayers help build a stronger spiritual defense.

Sometimes, the hardest part of a crisis is waiting on God's timing. You might feel like the struggle is dragging on, but remember, God's plan is perfect. He knows exactly when and how to bring you through.

Isaiah 55:8-9 (NKJV) reminds us of God's wisdom:

"For My thoughts are not your thoughts, nor are your ways My ways," says the Lord. "For as the heavens are higher than the earth, so are My ways higher than your ways, and My thoughts than your thoughts."

Trusting God's timing means staying patient and steadfast, knowing that whatever you're going through will ultimately show you more of God's power and purpose.

Conclusion: Victory Within the Hedge

Guarding the hedge during a crisis isn't easy, but it's doable with faith, prayer, fasting, and reliance on God's strength. Remember, you're not fighting this battle alone; God is right there with you, and your community of believers is lifting you up.

As you face crises, let these challenges make your faith stronger and deepen your trust in God. Know that inside the hedge of His protection, you're safe, no matter what's happening around you. Stand firm, keep your hedge guarded, and watch God bring victory into your life.

CHAPTER TWELVE

LIVING IN THE OVERFLOW OF GOD'S PROTECTION

EXPERIENCING THE OVERFLOW

I n this final chapter we are going to review and summarize some points from the other chapters.

The Abundant Life

Jesus set the stage for what abundant living looks like in John 10:10(NKJV):

"The thief does not come except to steal, and to kill, and to destroy. I have come that they may have life, and that they may have it more abundantly."

Living inside God's hedge sets you up to receive this abundant life. It's a life where God's blessings aren't just enough; they're more than enough. And this abundance goes way beyond material things; it's about spiritual riches like peace, joy, wisdom, and strength that overflow into every part of your life.

God's blessings aren't meant to be kept to yourself; they're meant to be shared.

Paul breaks it down in 2 Corinthians 9:8 (NKJV):

"And God is able to make all grace abound toward you, that you, always having all sufficiency in all things, may have an abundance for every good work."

Sharing the overflow means being generous; with your time, your resources, and your gifts. It means letting what God has poured into you pour out to others, whether that's by giving, encouraging, or simply being present for those in need.

Living with a Heart of Gratitude

Gratitude is the natural response to living in God's overflow. When you start recognizing all the blessings in your life, your heart can't help but be filled with thanks and praise for what God's done.

1 Thessalonians 5:18 (NKJV) keeps it simple:

"In everything give thanks; for this is the will of God in Christ Jesus for you."

Gratitude shifts your perspective. Instead of focusing on what you don't have, it reminds you of all that God has provided. It keeps you humble, acknowledging that every good thing you've got comes straight from God.

Maintaining a Spirit of Worship

Worship is a lifestyle. Living in the overflow of God's protection should naturally lead you to a life of worship, where everything you do reflects your love and reverence for God.

Paul challenges us in Romans 12:1 (NKJV):

"I beseech you therefore, brethren, by the mercies of God, that you present your bodies a living sacrifice, holy, acceptable to God, which is your reasonable service."

Being a "living sacrifice" means your whole life; your actions, your decisions, your thoughts; are all dedicated to glorifying God. Worship isn't just about singing; it's about how you live, work, and interact with others, showing God thanks for His protection and blessings every day.

Impacting Others Through Your Overflow

Living in God's overflow gives you the chance to impact the lives of those around you. Whether it's through kindness, sharing your story, or just being a godly example, your life can inspire others to seek God's protection and experience His overflow too.

Jesus says it like this in Matthew 5:14-16 (NKJV):

"You are the light of the world. A city that is set on a hill cannot be hidden. Nor do they light a lamp and put it under a basket, but on a lampstand, and it gives light to all who are in the house. Let your light so shine before men, that they may see your good works and glorify your Father in heaven."

Your life, lived in the overflow, becomes a light that points others to God. People need to see the peace, joy, and abundance that comes from living under God's hedge, they'll be drawn to seek that same blessing in their own lives.

Living with Expectation

Living in the overflow also means having a mindset of expectation; expecting God's continued provision and guidance. It's not about being entitled but about trusting that God is faithful to His promises. Expectation keeps you looking forward, knowing that God's best is yet to come.

Philippians 4:19 (NKJV) gives us this assurance:

"And my God shall supply all your need according to His riches in glory by Christ Jesus."

This promise reminds you to live with confidence, knowing that God's resources are limitless and He delights in taking care of His children.

Conclusion: Walking in the Fullness of God's Blessings

As we close this journey through the principles of God's hedge of protection, remember this isn't the end; it's just the beginning. Now you've got the tools and understanding to live a life that invites God's presence, guards His protection, and overflows with His blessings.

Living in the fullness of God's blessings means embracing gratitude, keeping a heart of worship, and expecting God to keep showing up. It's about sharing what God's given you, making a difference in the world, and always pressing closer to Him.

By doing this, you won't just experience the abundant life Jesus promised; you'll be a blessing to everyone you encounter, helping them find their way to God's protection and His overflow too.

May your life shine with the peace, joy, and security that comes from living within God's hedge. Walk confidently in His blessings, knowing He is your protector, provider, and ever-present help in all situations. And as you live in this overflow, may you inspire others to seek the same, bringing them into the safety and abundance of God's amazing love and grace.

CHAPTER THIRTEEN

A POWERFUL PRAYER OF SALVATION

CLAIMING GOD'S PROMISE FOR NEW LIFE

Scripture Prayer Points:

> *Romans 10:9 (NKJV):* "That if you confess with your mouth the Lord Jesus and believe in your heart that God has raised Him from the dead, you will be saved."

- *John 3:16 (NKJV):* "For God so loved the world that He gave His only begotten Son, that whoever believes in Him should not perish but have everlasting life."

- *2 Corinthians 5:17 (NKJV):* "Therefore, if anyone is in Christ, he is a new creation; old things have passed away; behold, all things have become new."

Heavenly Father,

I come before You today, recognizing my need for You in my life. Lord, I'm tired of trying to do things my way, walking down paths that have led me away from Your presence. Today, I choose You. I choose life. I choose freedom. I choose to step into Your loving arms, knowing that You've been waiting for me all along.

Lord, Your Word says in *Romans 10:9* that if I confess with my mouth that Jesus is Lord and believe in my heart that You raised Him from the dead, I will be saved. Right now, Lord, I confess it—I declare that Jesus is Lord of my life. I believe that You sent Him to die on the cross for my sins, and that He rose again, defeating death and the grave. Thank You, Lord, for making a way for me to be saved!

Father, You said in *John 3:16* that You loved the world so much that You gave Your only Son so that whoever believes in Him would not perish but have everlasting life. I thank You for loving me that much, for seeing me in my brokenness and sending Your Son to redeem me. Lord, I believe in You. I believe in Your promise of eternal life, and I receive it right now in Jesus' name.

Lord, I'm laying down my past—every mistake, every failure, and every sin. I'm letting go of the old me. Your Word in *2 Corinthians 5:17* says that if anyone is in Christ, they are a new creation—the old things have passed away, and behold, all things have become new. I claim that promise today. I declare that I am a new creation in Christ. The old is gone, and the new has come!

Forgive me, Lord, for all my sins. Wash me clean with the precious blood of Jesus. I turn away from my old ways, and I turn toward You. I surrender my heart, my mind, and my spirit to You. Fill me with Your Holy Spirit, Lord. Empower me to live for You every day. Guide my steps, lead my decisions, and keep me close to Your heart.

I thank You, Lord, that my name is written in the Lamb's Book of Life. I thank You that I am now a child of God, no longer bound by sin but free to walk in Your light. Help me to stay on the path of righteousness, to seek You first in all things, and to grow in my relationship with You.

Thank You for saving me. Thank You for loving me. Thank You for giving me a hope and a future. I am Yours, Lord, now and forever. In the mighty name of Jesus, I pray, Amen.

CHAPTER FOURTEEN

A PRAYER OF REPENTANCE:

RETURNING TO GOD'S PROTECTION

Heavenly Father, I come before You with a heart that's wide open, knowing I need You now more than ever. Lord, I'm not coming with excuses; I'm coming with a heart that's ready to be real. I confess my sins, my shortcomings, and the times I've strayed outside of Your will. I'm laying it all at Your feet because Your Word says in 1 John 1:9, "If we confess our sins, He is faithful and just to forgive us our sins and to cleanse us from all unrighteousness." Cleanse me, Lord. Wash me in Your precious blood and make me whole again.

Father, I repent for every time I've ignored Your boundaries, for every moment I thought I knew better than You, and for the times I let pride, fear, or stubbornness lead me away from Your path. Your Word tells me in Isaiah 59:1-2 that my iniquities can separate me from You, but right now, I'm turning back. I don't want anything standing between us. I'm running back into Your arms, into Your grace, and into the safety of Your hedge.

Lord, I ask for Your forgiveness for every time I stepped out of line, for every moment I tried to do it my way instead of Your way. You said in Psalm 51:10, "Create in me a clean heart, O God, and renew a right spirit within me." Lord, create in me a heart that desires You above all else. Renew me, restore me, and set me back on the right path. I don't want to live outside of Your protection. I want to live inside Your will, where Your peace, joy, and blessings flow.

Father, I'm surrendering my pride, my plans, and my will. I'm choosing today to walk in obedience to Your Word. Your Word in 2 Chronicles 7:14 reminds me that, "If My people who are called by My name will humble themselves, and pray and seek My face, and turn from their wicked ways, then I will hear from heaven, and will forgive their sin and heal their land." Lord, I'm humbling myself before You. I'm turning from anything that's not like You, and I'm seeking Your face. Heal my heart, my mind, my soul, and my life.

I thank You, God, that You are not a God of condemnation but of grace. You are a God who welcomes me back with open arms every time I stray. I'm grateful that You're a God who restores, who rebuilds, and who renews. As I repent today, I'm reclaiming every promise You've made over my life. I'm walking back into Your hedge, knowing that in Your presence is where I belong. Thank You for being my refuge, my fortress, and my hiding place. In Jesus' mighty name, I pray. Amen.

Scripture Prayer Points:

- **1 John 1:9** – Confessing sins and receiving God's cleansing.

- **Isaiah 59:1-2** – Understanding that sin separates us from God's presence.

- **Psalm 51:10** – Asking God to create a clean heart and renew the spirit within.

- **2 Chronicles 7:14** – Turning from wicked ways, seeking God's face, and receiving His forgiveness and healing.

May this prayer be your turning point, your comeback, and your reconnection with the One who loves you more than you can ever imagine. Let God's grace cover you, His mercy renew you, and His love pull you back into the safety of His arms.

CHAPTER FIFTEEN

A PRAYER FOR RESTORATION

CALLING ON GOD'S POWER TO REBUILD WHAT'S BEEN LOST

Heavenly Father,

We come before You, God of restoration, God of second chances, the One who makes all things new. We stand on Your Word, knowing that when everything feels broken, You are the Master Restorer. We remember how You restored Job, how You gave him double for his trouble after he lost everything. Lord, You are the same yesterday, today, and forever. What You did for Job, You can do for us!

Lord, we call on You, as Your Word says in Joel 2:25 (NKJV):

"So I will restore to you the years that the swarming locust has eaten." Father, we declare Your promise over every lost year, every broken dream, every stolen opportunity. Restore the time, the joy, and the peace that the enemy thought he could take. We stand in faith, believing that You are turning things around even now!

Father, in Psalm 51:12 (NKJV), David cried out:

"Restore to me the joy of Your salvation, and uphold me by Your generous Spirit."

Lord, some of us have lost our joy, lost our peace, and lost our way. But we ask You, Lord, to bring back the joy of being in Your presence. Lift us up, God, by Your Spirit. Fill our hearts with hope, peace, and a renewed sense of purpose. Don't let us stay in this place of brokenness; take us higher!

Lord, You said in Isaiah 61:7 (NKJV):

"Instead of your shame you shall have double honor, and instead of confusion they shall rejoice in their portion. Therefore in their land they shall possess double; everlasting joy shall be theirs."

Father, we are claiming that double portion right now! For every tear we've cried, for every setback, for every door that was slammed in our faces, Lord, give us double. Let Your favor chase us down. Turn every loss into gain, every trial into triumph. We are believing You for that "double for our trouble," and we are not backing down!

Father, we declare like the Psalmist in Psalm 23:3 (NKJV):

"He restores my soul; He leads me in the paths of righteousness for His name's sake."

Lord, restore our souls! Restore our minds, our hearts, our spirits. Lead us back onto Your path of righteousness. Guide us in every decision, every step, and every move. Let Your name be glorified in our comeback story!

We come against every scheme of the enemy that's tried to keep us down. Devil, you thought you had us, but we serve a God who turns graves into gardens, who makes ways out of no way, and who speaks life where there was none. We rebuke every spirit of despair, every lie that says it's too late, and every stronghold that's tried to hold us captive. We declare freedom, restoration, and breakthrough in the mighty name of J esus!

Lord, we thank You right now, because we know that restoration is already in motion. We don't need to see it to believe it; we trust Your Word. You are the God who restores, who redeems, and who renews. So, we stand in expectation, praising You in advance for the restoration that's coming. We know You are faithful, and we are ready to walk in the overflow of Your blessings.

In the powerful name of Jesus, we pray, Amen.

CHAPTER SIXTEEN

A PRAYER FOR GOD TO STRENGTHEN YOUR HAND

SCRIPTURE FOCUS:

Isaiah 41:10 (NKJV): "Fear not, for I am with you; Be not dismayed, for I am your God. I will strengthen you, Yes, I will help you, I will uphold you with My righteous right hand."

Psalm 18:32 (NKJV): "It is God who arms me with strength, and makes my way perfect."

Philippians 4:13 (NKJV): "I can do all things through Christ who strengthens me."

Prayer:

Heavenly Father, I come before You right now, acknowledging that You alone are my strength and my shield. Lord, I need You today—I need You to step in and strengthen my hand, to give me the power, the courage, and the wisdom to walk the path You've laid before me.

Father, I stand on Your promise in Isaiah 41:10, where You told me not to fear because You are with me. You said You would strengthen me, that You would help me, and that You would uphold me with Your righteous right hand. So, Lord, I'm asking right now that You make good on Your Word. Strengthen my hand, Lord, for the battles I face, for the mountains I need to climb, and for the valleys I must walk through.

God, I declare that it is You who arms me with strength, who makes my way perfect (Psalm 18:32). When I feel weak, when my hands feel heavy, remind me that I don't stand on my own power but on Yours. Remind me that Your grace is sufficient and that Your power is made perfect in my weakness (2 Corinthians 12:9).

Lord, I know that apart from You, I can do nothing. But with You, I can do all things through Christ who strengthens me (Philippians 4:13). So right now, I lay my doubts, my fears, and my insecurities at Your feet. Strengthen my hand, Father, that I might hold on tighter to Your promises. Strengthen my hand, Lord, that I might reach out to others, lifting them up just as You have lifted me.

Help me, Father, to stand firm, to keep my hand steady on the plow, and to never look back (Luke 9:62). When the enemy comes in like a flood, I ask that You raise up a standard against him (Isaiah 59:19). Fortify me, Lord, from the inside out. Strengthen my hand so I can fight the good fight of faith, so I can press toward the mark, and so I can finish the race You've set before me.

And Father, even when the weight of the world seems too heavy, remind me that Your yoke is easy, and Your burden is light (Matthew 11:30). Teach me to rest in You, to lean not on my own understanding, but to acknowledge You in all my ways, knowing that You will direct my path (Proverbs 3:5-6).

Lord, I thank You in advance for the strength You're pouring into me. I thank You for the battles You've already won on my behalf and for the victories still to come. Strengthen my hand, Lord, so that in all I do, Your name is glorified. I pray this in the mighty name of Jesus. Amen.

CHAPTER SEVENTEEN

A PRAYER TO OVERCOME FEAR

STEPPING BOLDLY INTO GOD'S PROTECTION

Heavenly Father,

I come before You, recognizing that You are my refuge and my fortress, my God in whom I trust. Your Word says in Psalm 91:1-2 (NKJV), *"He who dwells in the secret place of the Most High shall abide under the shadow of the Almighty. I will say of the Lord, 'He is my refuge and my fortress; My God, in Him I will trust.'"* Right now, Lord, I choose to dwell in Your presence. I choose to abide under Your shadow where fear cannot overtake me.

Father, I rebuke every spirit of fear trying to take hold of me! Your Word declares in 2 Timothy 1:7 (NKJV), *"For God has not given us a spirit of fear, but of power and of love and of a sound mind."* I stand on that truth today. Fear has no place in my life because You have filled me with Your power, Your love, and a sound mind. I am not bound by fear—I am liberated in Your love.

Lord, let Your perfect love cast out every ounce of fear in my heart. Your Word says in 1 John 4:18 (NKJV), *"There is no fear in love; but perfect love casts out fear, because fear involves torment."* I don't have to live tormented, anxious, or afraid. Your love surrounds me, shields me, and drives away the fear that tries to consume me.

Father, give me the courage to stand firm in faith. Just like David, who faced giants and battles, I declare boldly as he did in Psalm 27:1 (NKJV), *"The Lord is my light and my salvation; whom shall I fear? The Lord is the strength of my life; of whom shall I be afraid?"* There is nothing too big for You, God. No situation, no enemy, no fear can stand against Your mighty power.

I claim Your promise of protection, Lord. You said in Isaiah 41:10 (NKJV), *"Fear not, for I am with you; be not dismayed, for I am your God. I will strengthen you, yes, I will help you, I will uphold you with My righteous right hand."* I stand on this promise, knowing that I am not alone. You are right here with me, strengthening me, upholding me, and helping me through every battle.

Teach me, God, to keep my mind fixed on You. Your Word in Isaiah 26:3 (NKJV) says, *"You will keep him in perfect peace, whose mind is stayed on You, because he trusts in You."* I shift my focus away from my fears and fix my eyes on You, the Author and Finisher of my faith. You are greater than every storm, and in You, I find my peace.

Help me to walk in boldness and not shrink back. Remind me that You have called me to be strong and courageous. As You spoke to Joshua, You speak to me: *"Have I not commanded you? Be strong and of* *good courage; do not be afraid, nor be dismayed, for the Lord your God is with you wherever you go.* "(Joshua 1:9, NKJV). I take this command to heart, Lord, and I choose courage over fear because I know You are with me.

Lord, let my heart be steadfast, trusting in You. Psalm 112:7 (NKJV) says, *"He will not be afraid of evil tidings; his heart is steadfast, trusting in the Lord."* Even when bad news comes or when the road gets rough, I will not be shaken. My trust is anchored in You, and my heart is secure in Your unchanging love.

Thank You, Lord, for breaking the chains of fear over my life. I step out today in faith, knowing that You are my shield, my protector, and my deliverer. I will not live in fear, but in the freedom of Your presence, with boldness, confidence, and unwavering trust in You.

In Jesus' mighty name, I pray, Amen.

CHAPTER EIGHTEEN

A PRAYER TO LIVE WITH ETERNITY IN MIND

Heavenly Father, we come before You with grateful hearts, knowing that our lives are but a breath compared to the eternity that awaits us with You. Lord, teach us to number our days, that we may gain a heart of wisdom (Psalm 90:12). Help us to see beyond the here and now, to lift our eyes from the temporary trials of this world, and set our focus on the eternal promises You have prepared for us. We know that this life is fleeting, but Your Word stands forever.

Father, we pray that You would keep us anchored in the hope of heaven. Remind us daily that we are citizens of Your Kingdom, and our true home is not of this world (Philippians 3:20). Let us live as ambassadors of Christ, representing Your light in every corner of this dark world. Lord, help us to walk with purpose, knowing that every step we take is leading us closer to You.

God, give us the strength to lay aside every weight and sin that so easily entangles us, and run this race with perseverance, keeping our eyes fixed on Jesus, the Author and Finisher of our faith (Hebrews 12:1-2). When the pressures of life try to pull us away, remind us that nothing compares to the glory that will be revealed in us (Romans 8:18).

Lord, let Your Word be a lamp unto our feet and a light unto our path (Psalm 119:105). Guide us by Your truth, that we might walk in obedience and stay within the boundaries You've set for our protection. Help us to store up treasures in heaven, where moth and rust do not destroy and where thieves do not break in and steal (Matthew 6:19-20). May our hearts always beat for You, and may we find our greatest joy in serving You.

Father, give us a heart that longs for Your presence above all else. When the world tries to distract us, draw us back to You. We declare that our lives belong to You, and we want to live each day with eternity in mind. Help us to be bold in our faith, quick to forgive, and eager to share Your love with those around us.

We thank You, Lord, for the promise of eternal life through Christ Jesus. We ask that You keep our minds set on things above, not on earthly things (Colossians 3:2). Help us to live each day as a reflection of Your glory, knowing that one day we will stand before You, and we want to hear those precious words, "Well done, good and faithful servant" (Matthew 25:23).

In Jesus' mighty name, we pray. Amen.

EPILOGUE

WALKING FORWARD IN GOD'S PROTECTION

As you close this book and prepare to continue your journey, remember that what you've learned here isn't just words on a page—it's an invitation to a deeper, more real connection with God. That hedge of protection He offers isn't just about keeping you safe from life's storms; it's a living, breathing sign of His love, His care, and His desire for you to stay close to Him.

Life's journey is full of highs and lows, joys and struggles, growth and setbacks. Sometimes, you'll feel God's hedge strong around you like a mighty wall, and other times, you might feel it's been lowered. But don't let that discourage you—remember, God is always in control, and His plans for you are always good, even when you can't see it.

Step into the journey with faith. Whether you're riding high in a season of blessings or pushing through a tough trial, know that God's got you. His presence is always with you, guiding you, protecting you, and pulling you closer to Him every day.

Keeping that hedge strong means depending on God every single day. And leaning on God isn't about being weak; it's about being wise. It's knowing that your strength, your protection, and your success all come from Him. So, stay connected. Make prayer, worship, and time in His Word a part of your everyday life. These are the tools that keep your hedge fortified, making sure you stay right in the center of God's will.

Every morning, take a moment to acknowledge God. Thank Him for watching over you, ask Him to guide your steps, and invite Him into every part of your day. Let your life be a daily "yes" to God's protection, trusting Him with everything you face.

As you live in the peace and safety of God's hedge, don't forget—it's not just about you. God's calling you to extend that same protection to others. Through prayer, encouragement, and just being there, you can help others find their way to God's safety.

Be that light in someone else's storm. Share what you've learned, lend a helping hand, and pray for those who are struggling. As you do this, not only are you strengthening your own hedge, but you're also building a community that lives under God's protective care.

Keep your eyes on the bigger picture. This hedge of protection we talk about is just a glimpse of the ultimate security we'll have in eternity with God. One day, there won't be a need for a hedge because we'll be right in His presence—no pain, no fear, no threats. But until that day comes, let the hope of heaven inspire you to live faithfully, knowing each step brings you closer to His promises.

A Final Prayer

As you move forward, take this prayer with you:

"Heavenly Father, thank You for Your unfailing love and protection. Thank You for the hedge You've placed around me, guarding my heart, mind, and life. Help me to live each day leaning on You, walking in Your ways, and welcoming Your presence into every part of my world. When I'm tempted to stray or when life gets tough, remind me of Your faithfulness and draw me back to Your safety. May my life shine as a testimony of Your goodness and be a light to those who need to find their way back to You. Guide me, protect me, and lead me into all the fullness of Your promises, now and forever. In Jesus' name, Amen."

About the Author

Michelle Barker

I am passionate about God and His people. With a heart full of compassion and a deep desire to see others thrive, my mission is to help believers grow, mature, and flourish in their walk with God. My heart beats to see people living in the fullness of God's abundance, standing firmly on His Word, and embracing their true identity in Christ.

Through my writing, teaching, and ministry, I aim to equip and encourage believers to stand strong on the promises of God. I believe that when we truly understand how much we mean to God, it transforms how we live, love, and serve. My greatest joy is seeing God's people live confidently in their purpose, rooted in His truth, and overflowing with His grace.

www.ingramcontent.com/pod-product-compliance
Lightning Source LLC
LaVergne TN
LVHW022341080426
835508LV00012BA/1297